HOW TO EQUIP THE AFRICAN AMERICAN FAMILY

Issues and guidelines for building strong families

**by
Drs. George & Yvonne Abatso**

**Edited with Bible applications by
Dr. Colleen Birchett**

A *umi* Publication
urban ministries, inc.
Chicago, IL 60643

Publisher
Urban Ministries, Inc.
1350 West 103rd Street
Chicago, Illinois 60643
(312) 233-4499

First Edition
First Printing
ISBN: 0-940955-17-2
Catalog No. 9-2734

Scripture quotations are from the King James Version of the Bible. Printed in the United States of America.

DEDICATION

This book is dedicated to Harvey and Cora Rollerson & Robert and Vicentia Abatso, our parents, who modeled the beliefs we share in this book.

CONTENTS

ACKNOWLEDGMENTS

We wish to acknowledge the outstanding contributions of publications manager and designer, Shawan Brand; copy editor, Mary C. Lewis; and wordprocessor Cheryl Wilson, without whose help the book could not have come into existence. Last, but not least, we wish to thank Media Graphics Corporation and Dickinson Press.

PREFACE

by Dr. Colleen Birchett

In the most recent issue of *The State of Black America,* published by the National Urban League, Dr. Robert Hill wrote an article identifying the most critical issues facing African American families by the year 2000. He states:

"After making unprecedented strides during the 1960's, black families experienced sharp social and economic setbacks during the 1970's and 1980's."

He went on to explain that the poverty rate for Black families rose from 20% of the population in 1969 to 30% of the Black population in 1987. Moreover, the unemployment rate rose from 6% in 1969 to 12% of the Black population in 1988. The most recent statistics provided by the National Urban League indicate that three times more Blacks are unemployed in 1988 than in 1969.

Hill described how economic instability has led to family instability and to other problems in the African American community, such as crime, gang violence, drug trafficking, homelessness, and general declines in living standards for Black families.

Crisis and stress are not new to the Black family. However, today problems such as these are forcing changes in both the structure and the functioning of African American nuclear families and their extended family networks. Historically, families facing such problems have formed and sought other African American families for help. In fact, most Black churches consist of networks of African American families, relating to one another in a type of extended family. Today, most of these extended families are hurting. However, the church can and has played a healing and supportive role in the life of the African American family.

Today, healing and supporting will require expanding the entire concept of family ministry, and being willing to incorporate new approaches that may be non-traditional in nature. It may also involve incorporating approaches which indeed are traditional, and which can be traced back to ancient African cultures.

This book is designed to help churches and individuals meet this challenge.

Purpose of the Book. The book is designed for people who are concerned about equipping and strengthening African American families. It is designed for people in local churches who are involved in ministries with families. This book is designed to equip the African American church to equip the African American families within the Black church and within the Black community. However, it can also be of benefit to individuals who seek to strengthen their own families.

Objectives of the Book. Upon completion of this book, the reader should be able to use the principles presented to minister to a variety of types of African American families, within their extended families. The reader should be able to recognize and discuss 12 aspects of African American family life, identify problems and challenges related to each aspect, and apply guidelines presented to ministering to African American families of a variety of structures.

The Content. The introductory chapter presents the African American family in its historical context, with a particular focus on the African past. It presents a number of values and practices embedded in ancient African cultures, explains how these values and practices are supported by Scripture, and illustrates how these values and practices can be restored to modern African American family life.

The first three chapters deal with the changes that have taken place in African American families in recent decades. Chapter One gives an overview of these changes. Chapter Two focuses on issues facing different types of two-parent families and couples, while Chapter Three focuses on issues facing different types of single-parent families. Chapters Four through Eleven deal with a variety of aspects of African American family life, and the related issues facing modern families and their extended family networks. Chapter Twelve focuses on African American family ministry in the local church.

An extensive bibliography contains books, periodical articles and resources that can be consulted for information and assistance in ministering with African American families. Quite a few of the books, dissertations, periodical articles and resources contained in the bibliography are by African American specialists, writing about the African American family.

The Organization of the Book. With the exception of the introduction, each chapter is divided into two parts. Part One begins with an African proverb, and a short vignette (or case study) of a typical African American family problem. This is followed by an exploration of the issue with which the chapter deals, along with related principles and guidelines.

Part Two of each chapter, titled, "Bible Families" provides the reader with the opportunity to examine one or more biblical families who were involved with the issue with which the chapter deals. Three types of exercises are included. The first type of exercise is an exploratory exercise. Five exploratory exercises per chapter provide the reader with the opportunity to locate additional information about the family from the Bible, to abstract principles from the lives of the biblical families involved, and to apply these principles to modern African American family life.

The second type of exercise is titled a "Family Ministry Application." This exercise allows the reader to apply the information gained in the chapter and the exploratory exercises to the development or improvement of a family ministry based in the local church. The third type of exercise allows the reader to make a personal application of the information.

Uses. This book can be used for private as well as group study. It can be used during Sunday School, as an elective. It can be used during training hour, to train all church workers and "bench members." The book also can be used during weekday Bible studies as a Bible study guide, and it can be used in family devotions. In fact, the book also may be used as the foundation for a church-wide retreat.

A separate Leader Guide illustrates how the book can be used in group study.

Private Study. If used as a private devotional guide, it might be useful to spread the material out over weeks or perhaps months. Select a different chapter each week or month. Then select different exercises each day until the exercises for a given chapter are exhausted.

Once all of the chapters are completed, it might be useful to read additional books and periodical articles from the bibliography at the end of the book. These books can be used to extend group or private study. They can provide additional information and support as the reader continues to minister to African American families.

Group Study: 90-Minute Sessions. The book is designed for a two-part group study session. Part One would be a time when participants, under the direction of a group leader (or minister), study Part One of the chapter, along with the scriptural passage presented. This initial study session would require about 30 minutes. Then the group leader would begin the "laboratory" session. In the laboratory session, the group would, collectively, investigate the biblical families presented at the end of each chapter.

The group study session is designed so that every person can contribute something to the understanding and application of the principles covered in the chapter. This process would begin as the group leader divides the larger group into five smaller groups. Each small group would be assigned a separate exercise from the set provided with the case study.

A small group leader would be appointed or elected for each small group. Within the small groups, the small group leader would assign one question (or two, depending on the size of the group) to each participant. In the event that there are more participants in the small group than there are questions, then people might work on questions in two's, three's, or more.

About ten minutes should be allowed for each small group participant to answer the question assigned to him/her. Then another ten minutes should be allowed for participants to present their answers to their small group. The remainder of the time should be spent allowing each small group to discuss the "summary question," the last question of each exercise.

At the end of the small group discussions, the smaller groups would reconvene with the larger group. In the larger group, a spokesperson from each of the five smaller groups would summarize their small group discussion. Then the larger group, under the direction of the original leader, would discuss the final "Family Ministry Application" and "Personal Application" at the end of each chapter.

Group Study: 60-Minute Sessions. In shorter periods, it might be necessary to use part of a given chapter as a stimulus for discussion during the group meeting itself. Then the other part of the chapter might be used as a "homework" assignment or for private devotional study.

Family Devotions. During the week preceding the study of a given chapter, all members would read a given chapter privately, along with the "Bible Family Study" at the end of the chapter. Each member would select a different related "fill-in-the-blank/discovery" exercise and, on the basis of it, prepare a short presentation for family devotions.

The devotional period would begin with a discussion of the points the authors make in the chapter. Then the "Bible Family" case study would be read. Each member would present insights based on the exercise (related to the case study) that they completed during the week. After each member has contributed, then the family, together, would discuss the "Family Ministry Application" and "Personal Application" at the end of each chapter.

In summary, the book can be used in many ways. However, the main purpose is that African American families everywhere become equipped to deal with the main issues currently facing families, and develop a closer relationship with the Lord Jesus Christ.

INTRODUCTION

"We cannot move ahead until we've looked behind."
(African Proverb)

Today, as in former days, the African American church is at the forefront of ministry with African American families. However, the African American family is in a crisis state. Many of the grim statistics are now well-known. In spite of the urgency of the situation, the place to begin developing a ministry to African American families is not necessarily with further experimentation and research.

The place to begin equipping the African American family is with a return to the basics—to cultural and spiritual principles that are rooted in the ancient African cultural past. No culture comes as close to the cultures depicted in Scripture as African cultures. The church needs to examine ancient African cultures in the light of Scripture, and determine whether, by restoring certain aspects of it, the African American family can be equipped to overcome the dilemma it now faces.

This introductory chapter first considers the African American family in Africa and during slavery. Then it considers the problems facing African American families today. Finally it presents the components of traditional African cultures which need to be restored to the African American culture.

The introductory chapter will serve as a backdrop against which the principles presented in future chapters can be considered.

The Historical Black Family. African American families have been fractured and broken since almost 400 years ago, when more than 100 million Africans were pulled from the bowels of Africa in despair and forced into slavery. The dilemma Black families face today began then. It began when African families were pulled from their native cultures.

Contrary to what is reported in many history books, Africans arrived from civilized societies. These Africans were ripped out of the cradle of civilization. In fact they were brought here from the land where humankind began. The most recent biblical and scientific research supports this fact. Scientists are now presenting evidence that all races originated from a small-framed Black woman who lived in the northern part of Southeast Africa. (*Newsweek,* Jan. 11, 1988)

The 100 million Africans were kidnapped and brought to America from a land which had the oldest universities in the world and the most advanced forms of technology of the ancient classical world. The great pyramids which stand on the lands of the ancient Africans attest to this fact. These pyramids, engineered and constructed 5,000 years before the birth of Christ, are still standing. They are so well-constructed that it is impossible to slip a sheet of paper between the stones out of which they are constructed.

On the walls of Egyptian tombs are the writings of the cultures and the descriptions of the early African way of life. These are still readable today. The slaves who were brought to America from Africa are from a people who started mathematics. It was there that science began. The historical Black family was a family rooted in a community. The community was rooted in a culture consisting of an extended family. Strong males were always available. People lived disciplined lives, in community. The historic Black family consisted of creative, resourceful people.

The Black Family During Slavery. Because African people have been a creative people, enslaved African people were also creative in selecting strategies for coping. Under slavery, Black people in America developed three major coping strategies to survive. One was to strengthen the extended family. That is, regardless of whether one is a biological relative, one could be incorporated into a given family. The other was to promote a strong sense of cooperation. Every Black person was part of a group.

The third coping strategy was to develop a strong Black church. During slavery the African American church helped Black families maintain hope. The church helped family members affirm their sense of self. It gave them an outlet for their

14

frustrations and it encouraged them to press on. Rituals, symbols, and secret communication all contributed to maintaining some residues of our culture and collaborating in our escapes to freedom.

The Black Family Today. As was predicted by Black sociologist Franklin Frazier in 1939, the Black family has undergone many changes. As he predicted, Black people have migrated from the South in large numbers, into the northern cities. With this movement has come a deterioration in family life. There has been a change in the role of the Black church and the role of the extended family. Many families have pulled away from the church.

With the move from a rural to urban setting, families have come to regard the church as irrelevant. Many complain that the church needs to be updated to meet the needs of modern Black people. They say that, otherwise, the church can't function as a major resource for assisting people in adjusting to modern life.

The extended family also has changed. One reason is that, as people moved, sometimes family members moved to different locations. For example, while part of a family went to California, another part may have moved to Chicago, and another part may have moved to New York, and so on. Or, some family members moved North while other relatives remained in the South. Families also have begun to assimilate into the mainstream of American life and consequently have experienced many of the tendencies other American families have felt, such as isolation from elder relatives and infrequent contact with elders' traditions and beliefs. All of these factors have contributed to the deterioration and disorganization of the Black family.

Today's Black family finds itself in a dilemma due to both external and internal factors, and the family is in a crisis. Statistics reflect trends in the condition of African American families. From 25 to 30% of all young Black males are either in prison or on probation, but supervised by the courts in some way. That is, at least 1/4 of Black youth are in jail or under the control of the judicial system. About 75% of African American children are being raised in poverty. Before Black babies are born, during the pre-natal stage and throughout the first two years of life, the level and type of nutrition is directly related to their brain development. Many suffer from poor nutrition, and can be expected to develop related problems. Nutrition will affect their development in infancy and their ability to profit from schooling.

Another factor affecting African American families is divorce. One out of three Black marriages ends in divorce. This adds to the number of families in which children will be reared by single parents. This also will affect their well-being, seeing that, whether Black or white, single parents are at the bottom of the poverty scale.

The gap between the poor and rich is widening. Moreover, during the past ten years, there has been a reversal of federal support for social services, civil rights and human rights, and this has disproportionately affected Black families, many of whom need an expansion of opportunities and assistance.

Minorities as a whole, and Black people in particular are becoming a threat to America largely due to changing demographics and birth rates. Minorities (primarily Hispanics and African Americans) have high birth rates. The declining birth rate is primarily a phenomenon of white middle-income people. Black people have a birth rate of about three times that of whites. Hispanics have birth rates that are about five times that of white Americans.

By the year 2000 minorities will make up 1/4 of the population of the United States. In fact by the year 2010, the population of 50 of the largest cities in the United States will consist predominantly of non-white people. The implications for politics are great. If many of these young people drop out of school, they will not have employable skills. Therefore they will become a financial responsibility of those who are working. The elderly and retired whites will depend upon these young minorities to keep money in the social security system, and to keep retirement funds building, causing anxiety and concern for many. The interdependence of people and the growth of the non-white population leads to perceiving Blacks as threats. Black males, so needed to keep our families strong, are in particular victims of the system. Some males have abandoned the responsibility of manhood, while others have chosen criminal pursuits thereby shrinking the ranks of spiritually strong, economically independent male models.

The Dilemma of Today's Black Youth. Black young people in general are at risk. This is due to a number of factors. First of all, Black youth who are having problems lack a sense of connectedness to other people, the society and history. Connectedness is at the core of one's personality which guides, directs and assists a person as s/he makes decisions and carves out a purpose in life. It is very difficult for many youth to have a sense of connectedness, largely because they do not see a place or purpose for themselves in the world that seems inviting, challenging and attainable. Their lives are unstable due to poverty. Their communities are often filled with drugs. The images they see are often either ones with which they don't want to identify or influence them to behave self-destructively.

Black youth also lack a sense of uniqueness. A feeling of uniqueness is what an adolescent seeks while at the same time wanting a sense of belonging. Young people need to feel that they are special. One's specialness needs to be so special that others recognize it. It is part of the basis upon which one respects oneself. Young people come here as babies, without any self feelings. They develop a sense of self as they evaluate the perceptions of other people toward them. If they have fathers and mothers who call them ugly names, the name calling will prevent them from feeling a sense of respect.

If they go to school and find that the majority of the children in special education are of their race, this sends other negative messages to them. If they look at television and see negative images of Black males, or if they see African American males only as athletes, sports figures or entertainers, they draw other wrong conclusions. They may grow up without being able to develop a sense of specialness except in very limited arenas.

Young people also lack a sense of power. They need to feel that they can have some impact on the world. Instead Black young people usually feel invisible and powerless. That is because people see and hear them, but don't listen to them or understand them. Therefore they don't feel that they are special, or accountable or responsible for what they do.

Young people also need a sense of their value as well as a system of values. Both come through a personal relationship with God through Jesus Christ. It develops as a person takes on the characteristics of God. For them to develop a sense of value, children need to be taught right from wrong. Without a belief system to guide them, they will not know how to relate to themselves or other people.

One of the reasons Black young people are in a dilemma is that some Black families are no longer able to function in terms of their traditional responsibilities. What culture should they transmit to children that will produce mature, spiritual adults? They are finding it harder to help their children develop a sense of identity, specialness, or a sense of values. This dilemma is made more serious by the acknowledgment of the moral, spiritual and educational decline occurring in American society.

While many Black families are stable, strong, Christian and growing, others are not. While many Black adults are in job positions that they never had before, others are unemployed. Upper- and middle-income Black families have about the same birth rates as white families, while lower-income Black families tend to have more children as do other low-income families in American society. The people having the largest number of children are those who are least capable of providing for them.

As mentioned previously, one approach to dealing with the dilemma would be to restore to African American culture certain basic components of traditional African culture and systematically incorporate these into the Christian education program of the church.

African Cultural Component #1: A Harmony of the Sacred and the Secular. In traditional African cultures, the secular and spiritual were not separate. All of life was a walk with God. A walk with God was the objective of these cultures' curriculum.

It was the intent of the family, of business, and of medicine. Of course there was corruption and perversion, the same as exists in any other culture. However, ancient classic African cultures were integrated around the goal of spiritual transformation. Their goal was the creation of a certain type of person.

Today, African Americans need to return to a similar basic "curriculum." It is not enough to just produce honor students bent on a life of materialism with no obligation to others. African Americans need to restore Black culture so that religion is a way of life, with no

18

separation in terms of whether one is in the church or in the street. Both the church and the neighborhood would be seen as part of the community, requiring God-like behavior.

To tear down the dividing wall between the sacred and the secular, African Americans will need to resist the tendency of American culture to do just the opposite. Western culture attempts to pour Christianity into a predesigned mold, which permits individuals and a country to call itself Christian and yet practice aggression and injustice. In Western culture, rather than shift away from greed and profit motives, Christianity has been reworked so that there is a separation of the spiritual from economics, science, counseling and other aspects of life, which are considered "secular." This reworking was done to satisfy unregenerated people and has resulted in the practice of playing games with God rather than genuinely worshiping God.

An example of this practice is the tendency to develop formulas whereby a person merely confesses his/her sins, accepts Jesus Christ, is baptized, and memorizes a few Scriptures. They learn to quote a few key verses and then they try to look sanctimonious on Sunday morning and/or Wednesday night. However, their moral behavior during the week does not shift from seeking profit at the expense of others. The problem for American life and for African American family life today, is that there is no harmony between the spiritual and what are considered secular aspects of life.

Ancient African cultures were not like that. The spiritual infused every aspect of life. For example, places of worship were also schools. This idea needs to be restored to African American churches. African American churches do a wonderful job of appealing to the senses. However there is a need to appeal to the minds of people as well. In Africa, learning was not considered "secular," but instead was "spiritual." It was not a part of African cultures to be fearful of learning. In African cultures every place of worship had a library. The Hebrew synagogues as a center of the life of a people is another example. Learning was a way of life.

One of the main missions of the temple was to equip parents to function as parents. Children didn't begin learning to write with simplistic, isolated statements like, "See Dick! See Jane!

See Spot run!" They learned to read and write in response to the Word of God. The curriculum of the African American church needs to consist of the values, beliefs and truths that will be internalized in the lives of family members. Character-building should be the focus. In Africa, before a child could understand the holy teachings, it already had an effect on him/her through the modeling of family and community.

African parents learned to prepare their babies from the womb by praying, singing and surrounding them with that which is spiritual. Then, from its very first day on earth, the baby had an openness for coming to know God and for entering the community. This openness was reinforced throughout the educational system. Life was integrated around a clear purpose for being thereby facilitating a consistent, balanced life.

This is one example of how Africans merged what Westerners considered "secular" with what is spiritual so that the spiritual infuses every aspect of life.

African Cultural Component #2: Harmony Between Male and Female Roles. The American obsession with the issue of "who's the boss?" in family life, is not rooted in African cultures. In African cultures, there was always a male chief and a female queen mother. The one person who could dethrone the male chief was the queen mother. In African village life today, where the traditional African culture is most evident, male and female harmony is evident in a number of ways. For example, in village life, one almost never hears a baby crying. That is because it isn't exclusively the mother's responsibility to pick up the baby. Whoever is closest to the baby picks it up.

Some of this flexibility of roles carried over to African American life. That is, traditionally, among African Americans, whenever the father was unemployed, he cooked the dinner and did other chores, while, in many instances, his wife worked. Boys were trained to wash, iron and do household chores. However, the more we have assimilated into American culture, the more the issue of "who's the boss" has emerged, and more rigidity has set into the family. Rigidity can prevent African American families from being able to cope with the challenges they now face.

20

African Cultural Component #3: A Sense of Community. Throughout traditional African cultures, there was a sense of community or collaboration. No child, woman, widow or widower was ever alone. This is in direct contrast to the "me" society which has developed in America over the past 20 or 30 years. The traditional African cultural belief, "I am because we are," is more consistent with underlying principles of the Word of God which indicate, "We are members of one another" (Ephesians 4:25b).

African Cultural Component #4: Next Life Preparation. African cultures strongly emphasized next life preparation. Next life preparation is also emphasized in Christian theology. However, in Western culture, next life preparation doesn't appear to have much of an effect on behavior in this life. This was such a concern in traditional African cultures that the way money and time were used reflected the value that we would not be here forever.

Traditionally, Africans were aware and accepted the reality that the short period of time one remains in this life is just preparatory. Life was seen as one small part of a life cycle. From childhood, African American young people of today must be made aware of this fact. They should be made accountable for their time. They should be told to use this time and this preparation for life-long eternity with the Lord. To govern present behavior and prepare for the future, Africans adhered to several basic principles: truth, justice, righteousness, harmony, propriety and order. These principles are also found in the Old Testament. The focus was on character development and preparation for a future life.

The Role of the Church. The African American church must be willing to make some radical changes in its approach to ministering to African American families. Otherwise young people, in large numbers, will die prematurely (particularly those between the ages of 18-30), due to substance abuse, sexually transmitted diseases and such. The church must be willing to abandon the concept of the club that meets once each week. A radical restructuring of ministry is needed.

To develop a sense of community, churches must rethink the meaning of the Gospel. Ministering is more than telling a person to come forth and trust the Lord. That is only the individual's part. The church has the responsibility to nurture individuals who come forth and to discipline them in the Lord. This is particularly true of young people who come from families that can't supply the nurturing. The church must do whatever is necessary to avoid a type of conflict where middle- and upper-income African Americans become alienated from lower-income Black people.

Churches must be willing to become places of teaching. There must be an attempt to challenge the mind. The church must assume responsibility for the education of youth, ensuring that their education is proper education and that it is spiritual education at the same time.

The church must make an effort to build congregations that consist of both lower- and middle-income people. That will be difficult; it will require leadership, diplomacy and prayer. Lower-income people have gifts to offer middle-income people. Middle-income people have skills and expertise which they must share. It is not enough to attend Morehouse, Yale and the University of California in order to become well-paid lawyers and doctors, but not in order to give service to the community.

These principles need to be taught to our youth very early in life. Leadership must be servant leadership. There is a need for leadership which is not threatened by expertise or education. This type of leadership also demands a redefinition of the entire concept of what leadership is throughout the structure of the church.

Finally, churches also must foster unity, within and across congregations. So many congregations are too small to tackle the multitude of tasks that need to be completed, in order to adequately minister to the African American community. Churches must come together and place competition and superficial differences aside so that goals can be accomplished for African American people.

Summary. This introductory chapter has considered the African American family within traditional African cultures and as it occurred during slavery. It considered the dilemma facing African American families today, and presented components of traditional African cultures which need to be restored to African American culture in general, and to the family in particular.

This introduction can serve as a backdrop against which to consider other issues facing African American families, presented in the following chapters.

CHAPTER ONE

TODAY'S AFRICAN AMERICAN FAMILY

"A grass mat does not last like a bulrush mat: a grass mat will not bend; it breaks to pieces." (African Proverb)

Aunt Bea and Uncle Dan sat in the car with the car doors open, watching as the generations of Moores gathered for the family reunion. Bea remembered when she and Dan had gotten married. Dan had been the last of seven brothers to marry. All of the living brothers were still married, and she and Dan were about to celebrate their 40th wedding anniversary.

Aunt Bea couldn't help wondering whether Uncle Dan would be able to deal with the many changes that had now taken place in the family. As Christians, they didn't know whether they could relate to younger family members who did not attend church, and, to their knowledge, had not accepted Jesus Christ as Saviour.

Just then three great-nephews darted across the park behind their mother, Nancy. Nancy had never been married, and each of her children had different fathers. Aunt Bea was suddenly reminded of her niece Iris, Nancy's mother. She remembered how difficult it was for Bea's husband Dan to accept Iris's announcement that she and her husband Jim were getting a divorce.

Bea and Dan were even more disappointed when Nancy's sister Brenda divorced and remarried a widower, combining her family of two with his family of three children. "That's probably the reason why Chucky turned out the way he did," Aunt Bea thought quietly. Chucky, Brenda's son, was a homosexual who had died of AIDS the earlier part of the year. "None of this would have happened if Iris and Jim hadn't gotten a divorce in the first place," Bea went on thinking. "They should have stayed together for the sake of the children."

Just then Uncle Dan broke the silence. "You know, they told me Nancy's third baby is not her fault," he whispered. "They say she was raped." Just then Bessie, their oldest niece walked up. "Well, hello!" Uncle Dan shouted. "How you been doin'? Got married yet?" he teased. A disturbed expression came across Bessie's face. "Not yet," she said. "I haven't found Mr. Right."

Aunt Bea faked a smile, but thought, "How could anyone be 40 years old and not have found Mr. Right? She's got a doctorate, but no common sense. There is such a thing as too much education." She continued trying to smile as her thoughts wandered back to the family gathering in the park. "Probably at least half of them have illegitimate children," she thought, shaking her head.

The Moore family, in the above story, is not unlike many modern families today. Most extended families now consist of a variety of family types. People involved in family ministries need to take this into account. That is, if they are to help family members overcome some of the barriers that may separate them from one another and from the church.

However, in order to understand modern African American families, one must first examine the nature of the African American family. Then one must identify some of the pressures being exerted on the African American family today, and recognize the changes that these pressures are forcing African American families to make.

This chapter begins with a study of the nature of the African American family, focusing on various images of it that have been projected by sociologists. Then it describes pressures currently forcing changes in African American family life, and explains how those pressures may impact Black families in the future. Finally, it provides guidelines for churches and individuals who minister to African American families.

Images of African American Families. For the past few years, television, radio, magazines and newspapers have all carried information about the decline of the African American family. Such information has included the high teenage pregnancy rate, drug abuse, the very high divorce rate and a weak family life, even in homes of married couples. From these accounts, there appears to be an overall breakdown in communication among Black family members.

However, these negative images and prophecies about Black families are not new. As far back as the late 1930's, a prominent Black sociologist, E. Franklin Frazier, made some predictions about the Black family. He predicted that the Negro family, as he referred to it at that time, was in a "travail of civilization." Its probable future course would be increasing disorganization. He said that the desire for better jobs and freedom would move the southern agricultural Black society (in which most African American families were once found) into cities and towns. This would crowd them together into specified areas of cities.

Heads of families would experience difficulties in locating employment. Throughout this process of migration, African Americans would be disconnected from family roots, and from the Black church. Moreover, there would be a worsening condition of poverty. Quite a bit of what E. Franklin Frazier wrote is now evident among working class and poor Black Americans.

Daniel Moynihan, a white legislator writing as a sociologist in the 1960's, presented another image of the Black family. His image has come to be known as the pathological view of the Black family. He presented this view in his "Moynihan Report," describing the Black family as a family of pathology. He said that the matriarchal nature of it made it dysfunctional. It did not work as well as the white family structure because the structure of it was female-headed.

However, other authors have presented a different, more positive view of the Black family. Some of these authors wrote in response to Moynihan's report, being commissioned to do so by the National Urban League. Roy Hill, one of those authors, published his analysis in the book, *The Strengths of Black Families*. Hill emphasized the resiliency of Black families, their ability to bounce back after crises and endure difficulties. He emphasized the ability of Black families to adapt to various cultural demands.

In Black families, Hill found flexibility in the willingness to accept various roles depending upon need and circumstances. For example, male family members would often assume responsibilities for tasks which the larger society traditionally ascribed to females. If a man was unemployed, the woman in the family worked, without necessarily removing headship from the man. Children also were seen assuming responsibilities for tasks simply because the tasks had to be done. Therefore the children became more independent and more reality–oriented than children in other circumstances.

Hill also pointed to the high achievement orientation of Black families. His observations have been supported by formal research studies. Black families were found valuing educational achievement, even when they lacked the opportunity to acquire an education. This is largely because education remained the primary route by which Black people entered the mainstream of American life and improved their economic condition.

Hill also described the strengths of the extended Black family. He found it to consist of a large group of people committed to one another, sharing similar values and supporting one another with finances, problem solving skills, hope and encouragement.

Hill also found the Black church as a major resource for Black families. In fact Black families had a strong religious orientation which offered them a reason and hope for living. Their relationship to God was personal and experiential, a source of strength, and the primary means by which they endured life's hardships.

Pressures Forcing Changes in African American Family Life. Over the last 25 years, societal changes and value changes have affected American people in general, regardless of race. Some Black people have been in the best condition to respond to these conditions while others have been in the worst condition to respond to these changes.

One change has been the increase in the amount and kind of education necessary to obtain employment. Many Black people took advantage of educational opportunities made available during the late 1960's. During that time, there was a 200–300% increase in the number of Black students enrolled in colleges. Large numbers of these students completed college, and large numbers completed graduate school. It is these people who later acquired stable positions in the job market.

However, there are also those who are in the worst condition to cope with the new demands of the workplace. These include people who dropped out of school. High school drop–outs are often seen hanging around on street corners. They are young and they are middle–aged, but, if current trends continue, people in both of these age groups will never have full–time employment. These are the people living on the lower rungs of the economic ladder; they make up a permanent underclass.

27

In the area of education, the Black family also faces a real dilemma. According to current trends, fewer Black students will be in college in 1991 than were enrolled in 1990. While between 1960 and 1976, there was a 245% increase in the number of Black people enrolled in colleges, between 1976 and 1982, the percentage dropped by 6% and has continued to decline.

The decline of Black males completing college has reached the critical stage with more being under the jurisdiction of the courts and criminal system than in college. This further increases the educational gap between black males and females. The quality of education and collaboration between home and school is critical to the viability of the African American community.

Today, one out of two marriages will end in divorce, plunging many women into poverty. Instead of two people working together to maintain a household, there is often only one. Consequently, there is now the feminization of poverty. Almost 1/4 of female households who work full time fall below the poverty level of $10,000 per year. Moreover, fluctuations in the economy have closed many jobs and entire industries permanently, leaving people both unemployed and unemployable. There is a growing underclass in America, containing a high percentage of Blacks and minorities who will never have a full-time job in their lifetimes. Think of the impact that condition alone will have on Black family life.

Earlier it was stated that another factor affecting a large percentage of Black families was the absence of males as the heads of households. Now there is an even greater need for the presence of strong, spiritual Black males available to our youth as models of manhood. There has been a dramatic increase in the number of women who head their homes and are parenting alone. These include women who have been divorced and women who have never married. Women who have never married, but who have children, constitute about 3/4 of the holders of minimum-wage jobs in the United States. These women may work full time for one year, but may end up earning less during that year than what the United States defines as the poverty level for that year.

Economic realities have really affected Black families much more extensively than many of us will ever fully understand. If there is an 8% increase in inflation, a family which in 1990 earned $30,000 per year, will need to earn $80,000 per year in 2005 in order to maintain a way of life that is even remotely similar to the way of life that family lived in 1990.

African American families are disproportionately represented at the lower end of the economic ladder. At least 44% of Black families are headed by females, compared to 13% for white households. Seventy-five percent of Black children under six are raised in poverty. The average Black child can expect to spend more than five years of his childhood in poverty as compared to ten months for the average white child.

However, two out of every three females having their first children are single. These birth rates are escalating among low-income African American families, while birth rates, in general, are declining among Black and white middle-income families. For lower-income African Americans, the birth rate is three times higher than that of the overall population. Most of these are teenagers who are becoming parents before they are fully adult themselves.

If present birth rates continue among African Americans and Hispanics, by the year 2000, Blacks and Hispanics will comprise 1/4 of the U.S. population. Moreover, by the year 2010, it has been predicted that ethnic and racial minorities will comprise the majority population in more than 50 American cities.

The graying of America is also having an impact on the African American family. Our population has become older with a longer retirement life and expensive health needs. There are more older women and these women comprise a large percentage of those who live in poverty. Middle-aged offspring are having to care for grandchildren while at the same time caring for elderly parents and relatives. In fact the two largest groups among the poor are young minority children and older women.

Other factors having an impact on the Black family are high technology, automation, inflation, and geographic mobility. All of these have affected family life in America, but there has been a disproportionately negative effect on the Black family. We are in a transitional stage, and there has been a major shift in our society which will have reverberations throughout all aspects of our lives.

The Future Impact of Current Trends. Probably the most dramatic impact that current trends may have on the future of Black families is that all of them will not look alike. Their structures will differ, while their functions may remain the same. Consequently there will be a shift in focus from structure to function, or process.

That is, families will be less concerned with whether the head of the home is male or female, and more concerned with whether the family (regardless of who is head) meets the holistic needs of individual family members and adequately prepares its youth for full participation in adult life.

As far as education in Black families is concerned, if current trends continue, there will be limited access to higher education, due to increasing tuition rates and more exacting admissions requirements. Admissions will be determined more and more by test scores. There will be a greater need for child development centers which begin educating children and parents very early in life. Better quality preschools also will be needed.

The most critical issue facing families is their ability to transmit a set of values to their children which transcend those offered by Western culture—namely materialism. African American families will require a renewal of living, personal faith in God which will permeate all of their beliefs, decisions and behavior.

Guidelines for Ministering to African American Families. Two major stress absorbers traditionally have assisted Black families in coping with limited resources: the extended family and the Black church. These institutions can continue to absorb stress in the future if they reorder their priorities and accept the responsibility. These two support systems can be invaluable to those who want to reach Black families for Christ, and equip them for survival and service.

However, if major intervention from within the Black community does not occur, the future does not seem very bright for most lower-income Black families in particular. This is because it will be comprised largely of Black children, female-headed families, the uneducated, and overburdened older women. Increasingly serious economic realities may cause Black women to be less and less in a position to carry out their traditional functions of Christian nurturing and preparing family members for the world.

The family is critical for the survival of a people. Consider that the family is the first set of people with whom a child has continuous contact. That family is not just a passive transmitter of the culture to its children. It plays an active part in helping its young form a world view, and in forming attitudes about the self, others and life. It helps the child discover his/her place in the world. It accomplishes this by the activities in which the child engages and through its communication and example to the child.

The family introduces the child to the world of relationships, personal relationships. It demonstrates how people treat each other. Whatever happens in the future life of the child outside of the family is superimposed on those beginning experiences, attitudes, beliefs and expectations about self, others, the world, and God, which one learns within the family. It is also the place where the child develops an understanding of his/her mission in the world.

Churches and individuals who minister to Black families must equip families to continue protecting, nurturing, instructing and preparing their children for adulthood and Christian service. Churches must be willing to do this, regardless of a family's structure. Function rather than structure should become the focus of ministry as God's people reach out to disciple and assist families in need.

Summary. This chapter has provided an overview of the nature of the contemporary African American family. It also provided an overview of pressures impacting African American families and how those factors may impact Black families in the future. It also provided guidelines for ministering to Black families.

Although this chapter has presented some very grim realities, this should not discourage but rather encourage and guide those who minister to and/or are a part of a Black family. One must remember that Black people, because of their historic strengths, because of the heroic strengths of the extended Black family, and because of the outstanding witness of the Black church, has been able to survive in the past. This flexibility, resiliency, clarification of values, and commitment to God will enable Black families to continue surviving, in spite of pressures now bearing down upon them.

The challenge is for Christians to view ministry to church and unchurched families as a vital part of their discipleship and service to God through following the example of the wounded Saviour touched by the needs of His people.

Following is an exercise which provides the opportunity to apply some of the insights of this chapter to an analysis of some Black families in Scripture.

The introductory African proverb is from the GA language. GA or ACCRA is a West African language spoken in the eastern portion of Ghana, between the Volta River on the East and the Akwapim mountain-mass to the North and Northwest.

BIBLE FAMILIES

INSTRUCTIONS: The following exercises allow you to study a biblical family that faced pressure and was flexible enough to cope with it. The first five exercises consist of "fill-in-the- blank" questions, followed by a summary question. The sixth exercise allows you to apply the wisdom you gained from this chapter to the development of a family ministry in your local church. The seventh exercise allows you to make personal applications.

Elimelech

"Now it came to pass in the days when the judges ruled, that there was a famine in the land. And a certain man of Bethlehem-judah went to sojourn in the country of Moab, he, and his wife, and his two sons. And the name of the man was Elimelech, and the name of his wife Naomi, and the name of his two sons Mahlon and Chilion, Ephrathites of Bethlehem-judah. And they came into the country of Moab, and continued there.

"And Elimelech Naomi's husband died; and she was left, and her two sons. And they took them wives of the women of Moab; the name of the one was Orpah, and the name of the other Ruth: and they dwelled there about ten years. And Mahlon and Chilion died also both of them; and the woman was left of her two sons and her husband.

"Then she arose with her daughters-in-law, that she might return from the country of Moab: for she had heard in the country of Moab how that the Lord had visited his people in giving them bread. Wherefore she went forth out of the place where she was, and her two daughters-in-law with her; and they went on the way to return unto the land of Judah.

"And Naomi said unto her two daughters-in-law, Go, return each to her mother's house: the Lord deal kindly with you, as ye have dealt with the dead, and with me.

"And Ruth said, Entreat me not to leave thee, or to return from following after thee: for whither thou goest, I will go; and where thou lodgest, I will lodge: thy people shall be my people, and thy God my God:

"Where thou diest, will I die, and there will I be buried: the LORD do so to me, and more also, if aught but death part thee and me. When she saw that she was stedfastly minded to go with her, then she left speaking unto her." (Ruth 1:1-8, 16-18, KJV)

1. A Family Changing (Ruth 1:1-18)

Over the years, the structure of Elimelech's family changed. From the above story, describe the different forms his family took as it changed.

a. the traditional two-parent family (Ruth 1:1-2)

b. the single-parent family (1:3)

c. the "couples without children" (1:4)

d. the extended family (1:4)

e. the blended family (1:16-18)

f. SUMMARY QUESTION: Can you identify any of the above types of family structures in your personal extended family and church? What is the ratio of families with traditional structures (two parents), to those with non-traditional structures (b, c, d, and e above)?

2. Pressures and the Family (Ruth 1:1-5)

Describe the pressures Elimelech's family faced and explain

their probable impact on family life.

a. famine (1:1)

b. migration (1:1)

c. the absence of a strong male head (1:3)

d. the shortage of Ephrathite women or men (1:4; Deuteronomy 23:3-4)

e. widowhood (Ruth 1:3, 5)

f. SUMMARY QUESTION: Are Black families in your church and community facing similar types of pressures? Explain how these types of pressures are impacting Black family life today.

3. Stress Absorber #1—The Extended Family (Ruth 1:4-18; 2:5-20; 4:9-17)

The extended family played a major role in helping Naomi, Ruth and Orpah cope with the pressures they faced.

a. What is the first evidence of the extended family serving as a resource? (1:4-7)

b. What is the second instance of the extended family serving as a resource? (1:16-18)

c. What is the third instance in which the extended family served as a resource? (2:5-20)

d. What is the fourth instance of the extended family serving as a resource? (4:9-13)

e. What is the fifth instance of the extended family serving as a resource? (4:14-17)

f. SUMMARY QUESTION: Consider your extended family. What are some ways in which it has served as a resource to members of the family?

4. Stress Absorber #2—A Relationship with the Lord (Ruth 1:6, 16-22; 4:13)

It is evident that, in the midst of their trying circumstances,

Elimelech's family had faith in the Lord.
a. What evidence is there that Naomi had faith in God? (1:6)
b. What effect did Naomi's faith have on other members of her family? (1:16)
c. What is one way the Lord demonstrated that He would take care of Naomi? (1:16-17)
d. What is another way the Lord demonstrated that He would take care of Naomi? (1:20-22)
e. What is a way the Lord demonstrated that He would take care of Ruth? (4:13)
f. SUMMARY QUESTION: What are some ways the Lord has demonstrated that He would take care of you and other members of your family?

5. Flexibility (Ruth 1:1-6; 2:5-7; 4:9-10, 15-17)

Elimelech's family was flexible in dealing with pressure.
a. What is one way in which the family was flexible? (1:1-4)
b. What is a second evidence of flexibility? (1:6)
c. What is a third evidence of flexibility? (2:5-7)
d. What is a fourth evidence of flexibility? (4:9-10)
e. How did the Lord Himself demonstrate flexibility in His care for the family? (4:15-17)
f. SUMMARY QUESTION: In what ways has your extended family demonstrated flexibility in dealing with pressures it has faced? Are there families in your church which have demonstrated similar strengths?

6. FAMILY MINISTRY APPLICATION

In what specific ways can your church develop programs and activities to meet the needs of non-traditional family structures (single parents, widows, blended families, extended families, couples without children). Describe how Black families are becoming flexible in order to deal with these pressures.

7. PERSONAL APPLICATION

Describe ways in which your extended family is changing, due to pressures being exerted upon it. Compare and contrast your family with the family of Elimelech.

TWO PARENT FAMILIES AND COUPLES

"Two eyes see better than one." (African Proverb)

Cynthia and Russell had been married for about two years, but they had never really resolved some of the problems related to their children from previous marriages. They also had in-law problems, and problems with the previous spouses. Russell's children, Alvin and Steffany were now teenagers, and this was the weekend that they were to spend with their father.

Cynthia's children, Katrina and Crystall were also teenagers. Katrina and Crystall sat listening, as the argument between their mother and stepfather heated up.

"Katrina and Crystall are Christians!" Cynthia yelled. "I don't want them listening to that rap music your kids bring over here."

"Oh, shut up! I'm tired of that mess. All you listen to is what that preacher tells you. I caught his son the other day riding down the expressway blasting some rap music. What do you think his kids do when he's not around?"

"Alvin and Steffany are a bad influence on Katrina and Crystall. If you don't watch them, they'll end up loose just like their mother!" she screamed.

"Listen, I'll raise my kids the way I want them raised. I'd rather have them listening to rap music around me than sneaking off and doing it," Russell yelled back.

> *"Well, that's not all," Cynthia continued. "Alvin*
> *acts like he might be in a gang, and Katrina told me*
> *that Steffany is on birth control. She said her mother*
> *gave it to her. I don't want Katrina hanging around*
> *girls Steffany's age who already use birth control!"*
>
> *Just then the telephone rang. "Mama, hi," Cynthia*
> *began. Russell interrupted, yelling in the background.*
>
> *"Tell her to stay out of my business! Do you hear? I*
> *married you, not your mother."*

Cynthia and Russell are in a non-traditional two-parent family. At the same time, they are a part of an extended family network. Blended families, the result of remarriage after divorce or widowhood, are just one of the many types of two-parent families which are a part of most modern congregations.

To minister to an African American family such that of Cynthia and Russell, one must examine the extended African American family which, in varying degrees, is still intact and where possible, utilize extended family networks to evangelize, heal and restore people to the Community of Faith. This chapter focuses on various two-parent African American family structures. The scriptural basis for ministering to a variety of family types will be presented, along with principles for helping dual parent families.

The chapter is designed for family members, for persons who minister to families through family ministries of the local church, and others who desire to equip the African American family for survival and service. The chapter will conclude with exercises which allows the reader to apply the principles presented in this chapter to the study of a biblical family.

Varieties of African American Families. As noted in the case study of Chapter One, the extended African American family includes a variety of family structures. There are traditional two parent families, consisting of a husband, wife and (in most cases) their children. Then there are single parent families. However, there are also single people without children who either have never married, are divorced, widowed, and/or even homosexual. These single people are also a part of the African American extended family.

None of the above categories of families are homogeneous. That is, each broad category of family can be broken down into subcategories. Each subcategory has a different type of history and structure which influences the way its functions are carried out. The psychological dynamics of each type of family are also different, and it is important to understand these dynamics when one is ministering to families.

For example, some homes consist of working parents who juggle time and tasks to parent children. Some consist of couples who are comfortable and compatible with each other, and can anticipate one another's thoughts. As economic conditions have worsened, there has been a return to the trend of adult offspring, often with children of their own, returning home to live with their parents.

One friend, who is a professional woman, lives alone, while another lives in a nearby household with three women, a mother and two daughters all representing three different generations. They live on the mother's retirement and the income of one daughter. There are families barely surviving on AFDC living in crowded, dangerous neighborhoods where weekends are spent dodging bullets. Some men are working two jobs to keep the family together.

Parents with youths have concerns about keeping them in school, keeping them goal-oriented and away from drugs, and helping them resist peer pressure. These are godly parents who are concerned about their children's and their grandchildren's spiritual lives. However there are also households with no faith or knowledge of God, who must survive from day to day with no meaning or purpose in life.

Human development specialists are yet to fully discover the long-term effects of homelessness on those families who have no permanent place to live. Thousands of Black children are in foster homes. Some of them have a marginal status while waiting to be adopted.

Varieties of Two-Parent African American Families. As mentioned previously, there are many types of two-parent families, each having a slightly different history and dynamic. You can recognize them in your congregation and in your neighborhood. The most traditional two-parent family would be the one in which the husband and wife married, remained married, and had children. A slight variation of this would be the husband and wife who married, remained married, but did not have children.

A second type of two-parent family would be the family in which one or the other of the parents was married before, and remarried after divorce. In some cases, no children are involved. In other cases children from previous marriages may become part of the newly formed marriage. If both the parents were married before, and both have children, it is possible that both sets of children become a part of the new household, resulting in what is called a "blended family."

Increasingly, more American families are of this variety which often involves bringing together children from different life-styles, values and loyalties into a reconstituted family with a new stepparent who may have mixed feelings about parenting a child whom s/he did not produce.

A variation of this second type of two-parent family occurs when one or both parents have been married before, and have children. However the children from the previous marriage do not become part of the newly formed household, but one or both parents must pay child support to a previous spouse for the care of those children as well as continue participating in the life of children from a former marriage.

The varied configuration of families which exists both within and outside of the church represents different issues which cause confusion and struggle within families. The conflicts which arise provide opportunities for ministering to these families.

One can turn to the Bible for insight and wisdom on contemporary problems. There one can locate guidelines and principles which one can apply to current situations. God's plan for family life is modeled on the marriage of a husband and wife who are people of faith. Both represent a mature stage of faith development in which the decision has been made to follow the Lord.

God's will for two-parent families is the union of man and woman cleaving together and becoming one flesh as stated in Genesis 2. This relationship involves commitment, intimacy and holiness. After commitment to God, there is commitment to one's mate. Therefore, husbands and wives become committed to the type of home they desire and to making it work. Becoming one flesh compels husbands and wives to grow in intimacy.

Each partner works at becoming compatible with the other. Each one becomes more whole as the two live in synchronized harmony with one another. One flesh implies not only physical intimacy but emotional and intellectual closeness. The relationship of husband and wife is an analogy of Christ's relationship to the church. As such, it is holy and clean.

Biblical Leadership. It is not surprising that the Bible provides a model for the family. This model, incidentally, can work in any institution, whether social or spiritual, where there is need for leadership. The model is taken primarily from Ephesians chapter five which calls for a leader, or head, and an assistant and subordinates.

The leader is the husband and the assistant and subordinates are the wife and children. The model is based on the recognition that the family must accomplish specific functions and needs to operate efficiently. This is not the relationship between all males and all females perse, but between husband and wife.

Husband and wife make up the basic social unit of human relations, and in societies, ancient or modern, roles are assigned to help the relationship function smoothly. However, in order to function well, any system or group has to have someone who is responsible for it. That is why the family, as a system, should have a head. In Ephesians, the fifth chapter, this concept is presented.

Christian headship is not the same as Eurocentric or secular headship. The very term, "leader" brings distorted and repulsive images to many people. The Christian concept of leader is not the manipulative, controlling dictator but the wounded healer who leads by example.

Even using the term "Christian" to describe the leadership of the husband does not produce the necessary understanding we need. Unfortunately the term has been used by evil people to foster self-interest to the extent that our sensitivities have been dulled.

Perhaps the best human illustration is the rulership of an African chief and that of the pharaoh of ancient Kemet (Egypt). Our ancestors gave testimony of God and manifested what they said of God in their lives. Their testimony was this: God revealed Himself to them in the foothills of the mountains of Mood (Mt. Kilimanjaro) and taught them how to live and how to relate to Him.

There were two parts to the daily manisfestation. One was that God created everything and therefore His Spirit was in all of His creations. The soil, trees, rivers, animals, sun, moon, stars, and all other things of which they were conscious, they treated with reverence. The second part of the manifestation is that man is a complex being with many aspects. He has emotions, drives, desires, natural and physical components. All of these components are more often than not at conflict with one another. The Spirit of God that dwells in man (the Egyptians called it the "Ka") must restore and maintain order in humankind. The pharaohs of Kemet and the chief in more recent times was to be an example for the people. As such the pharaoh's rulership was to demonstrate how each was to rule over himself. The pharaoh or the chief was trained from childhood to understand and know God, as well as to understand himself and his mission in life.

In the Christian family the leadership of the husband was based on the same principle. The husband is to demonstrate how each member of his family should live. He must first submit himself to the Spirit of God and allow God's Spirit to work through him to demonstrate how each member should live. The particulars are discussed as you continue reading this chapter.

The traditional chief in African culture has a powerful but responsible role. A chief must make decisions that are in the best interests of his people, therefore vision and wisdom are needed. His life is circumspect, open to public scrutiny at all times.

The ancient Egyptian pharaohs were also to show through their rule the character of God and by their rule teach that individual lives are the temple of God. They were respected and honored because they were people of good character. Their leadership was not differentiated into the secular and the sacred. All behavior and decisions were weighed by their fundamental calling to represent God-like character before the people.

Given this awesome responsibility of chieftancy or headship, the chief had helpers who offered advice and spoke for him. The queen mother also had a powerful role of demanding insight and wisdom as she arbitrated, mediated and counseled. She had the authority to question the chief and hold him responsible to his high calling, thereby maintaining the integrity and sanctity of the role.

When two people have accepted their rightful relationship to God and bring a willingness to work at obeying His commandments in relationship to each other, then the basis for trust and intimacy can flourish.

In Ephesians, the responsibility of the husband and wife is explained. Both husband and wife should be subjected to Christ first and then to one another. Because someone is the head doesn't mean the person makes decisions by himself. It doesn't even necessarily mean he has to handle the finances. The person in the family who is best able should be delegated that responsibility. Effective leadership requires good matching of people and skills to the tasks to be performed.

In any family, there ought to be consultation, cooperation and joint decision making. Effective heads do not handle themselves as autocrats. Managing a family is too complicated today for one person.

What, then, is the role of the husband? He is to love his wife even to the extent of dying for her. Anticipating how humans would distort the concept of love, God gave clear-cut guidelines in 1 Corinthians 13 on how love behaves.

Based on the Ephesians writer's comments concerning Christ's love for the Church, it follows that if the husband is to direct the family, he must be knowledgeable. If he expects allegiance from his wife, then he must fulfill his role as head. His love for her, then, demands that he see to it that his wife remains:

a) spotless and physically healthy

b) without wrinkle, emotionally and mentally

c) holy and spiritually sound

d) without blemish or damaged reputation

In other words, whatever decision the husband makes must be in the best and total interest of his wife. With this clear directive any head of a family will think very, very carefully before he decides to make a major decision or purchase. Serious consideration will be given to the family's needs for food, education, economic security, health care, emotional well-being and spiritual growth.

Economic security and good health require careful planning and wise decision making. The key to the success or failure of a marriage is how the husband and wife love, respect, and trust each other. Good mental and physical health also require planning. They do not happen by accident. God has given us remarkable factories, our bodies. The various sections of it continuously produce needed material for other sections.

However, like any other factory, the body has to be maintained and repaired. God also continues to give us knowledge to repair and maintain our bodies. However, in the United States, the repair and maintenance of our bodies is expensive. To maintain good health requires good planning and sensible living.

The husband's responsibility is to keep pace with the rapid changes in health care costs and plan to meet the cost of health care. Most medical insurance, for example, is not sufficient to meet the health needs of the average family. Therefore it is important to check the coverage and get supplementary coverage, when possible. It is far less expensive to get good insurance than to be in the hospital just once and have to pay a large portion of that bill.

The husband should also see to it that his family practices preventive health care. This includes regular physical checkups and exercise. If a wife can go to the beauty shop and pay $20 to $30 every two weeks, it is only sensible for the husband to see to it that she goes to see the doctor twice a year to maintain her health.

A family life is an enjoyable one. It is true we all make errors. Sometimes we make very foolish and expensive ones. However, there is nothing more joyful than regrouping as a unit, and charging forward again as a unit. To do this, both the husband and the wife need to be loved, respected, and trusted, but the husband must have love for his wife. He must have deep affection in order to make the wise and unselfish decisions which offer her full protection.

Biblical Submission. In response, the wife is told to respect, honor and praise her husband. This two-fold caring/sharing relationship is greatly needed in our homes. The relationship calls for the wife to submit herself to her own husband—even as she does to the

Lord. Notice that she is not asked to submit herself to just any man, but to her own husband. That is because her husband represents God as the leader of their little family organization.

The Bible indicates that the wife's submission should be in the same way as the church is subject to Christ. The leadership of the church comes from Christ. He gives direction to the church, and in order for the church to grow and maintain harmony it has to be subject to its Leader—Christ. Jesus points out that our relationship to Him is no longer as slaves but as friends (John 15:15). This is also true of the marital relationship.

This means the wife is to cooperate, complement and balance out the husband's inadequacies as a helpmate. At the same time it is her privilege to enjoy her husband's full protection and love. The duty cannot be performed without the privilege, and the privilege cannot be enjoyed without performing the duty. These guidelines are straightforward, and given in order to promote continuous growth in both husband and wife as they seek to obey God.

Challenges Facing Two-Parent Families. One set of challenges relates to the problem that occurs when one of the spouses is not a Christian. It is difficult enough to keep a marriage working when both partners are Christians, not to mention when one is not. The Bible is very clear about the fact that, fundamentally, we are to be united with people who are Christians. However, many women are in situations where they became Christians after they married, and their husbands did not. Under these circumstances the Christian member must reflect Christ and seek to establish the sanctity of marriage.

In other situations, women, because of the scarcity of men, marry someone who is not a Christian. The male shortage has gotten very critical for both young and mature, unmarried African American women. In fact, many have difficulty meeting eligible Christian males. It is so painfully lonely and difficult for many women who have been hurt and disappointed by men. Some women, out of desperation, get caught in a secular way of life in search of a husband and make poor choices which they soon learn to regret.

Another set of challenges relates to the situation in which a husband, while remaining physically present, does not take over as head of his family. When this happens, it forces the woman into the headship role or creates a vacuum of leadership in the home. This may lead to conflict when the husband begins to resent her authority and when the wife either becomes excessively domineering or longs for a role of interdependence.

Ministering to Two-Parent Families. The most common conflicts between husband and wife have to do with issues of intimacy and finances. Underneath is often the issue of power. In such instances, the counselor must help the couple understand the need to "flesh out" the meaning of this in their conflicts with each other.

If the husband abandons his responsibility, someone must take charge, particularly if the well-being of children is involved. If the husband relinquishes his role as head, should he not be willing to submit to his wife and allow her to function as the head? Otherwise, he must assume the position that God has given to him with love and kindness. She too must assume the gracious role of friend-wife.

Another challenge facing two-parent families is the case in which one or the other of the partners is not a Christian. In this case, prevention is more effective than an ounce of cure. The church and the family can engage in activities that amount to prevention. Both the church and the family can help single African American women by consciously matchmaking. Pastors and others can make it a point to help eligible Christians meet each other. Pastors and counselors also can do premarital counseling so that good marriages can be initiated within the church on a Christian basis, with the support of the Community of Faith, and with accountability to it.

The family and the church can work to prevent bad marriages from occurring by becoming more involved with the young people for whom they are responsible. For example, a father can determine that he will not give his daughter away unless he knows at the front end that he can hold the prospective son-in-law accountable for caring for his daughter.

In fact the family might begin a tradition in which the older relatives serve as advisers to the marriage. This only works if older members are themselves practicing biblical principles. Moreover, elders would let the prospective son- or daughter-in-law know that, if s/he enters the family, s/he can feel comfortable communicating with them about the well-being of the marriage. In fact the older relatives themselves would feel comfortable communicating with the married couple about how they can strengthen their marriage. This kind of exchange works only in relationships where this kind of communal caring has been agreed upon.

The rich, accumulated experience on how to create and maintain healthy family relationships can be passed on from one generation to another. If any young man or woman gets past this type of scrutiny, s/he would have to be serious in his/her intentions. S/he would certainly have the word up front of what would be expected. Our young people need help in making choices because they don't have many people from whom to select, and we need to help them locate potential mates who are Christian.

Non-Christian mates need to feel welcomed at the church's outreach ministries in the home. These should be designed for them. Nothing is more powerful than the Scripture lived out in the flesh over time to bring a person to Jesus Christ. African American men and women need to learn how to respect each other in words and deeds. Our self-esteem has been damaged by slavery and racism to the extent that we sometimes demean each other. It will take conscious effort and Holy Spirit empowerment for some to bridle their tongues and honor one another.

Summary. This chapter has focused on a variety of family structures within the African American community, with a particular focus on varieties of couples and two-parent families.

Problems faced by modern couples and by modern two-parent African American families were discussed, along with related biblical principles related to two-parent families. The chapter also presented guidelines for ministering to couples and families.

The following exercise provides the opportunity to apply the principles covered in this chapter to the study of a biblical family.

BIBLE FAMILIES

INSTRUCTIONS: The Bible contains a variety of two-parent families and couples, some of whose children are not mentioned. Within these families, wives assumed various roles. The following exercise allows you to study some of these families. The first five exercises consist of "fill-in-the-blank" questions, followed by a summary question. The sixth exercise allows you to apply the wisdom you gained from this chapter to develop a family ministry in your local church. The seventh exercise allows you to make personal applications.

Aquilla and Priscilla

"After these things Paul departed from Athens and came to Corinth: And found a certain Jew named Aquila, born in Pontus, lately come from Italy, with his wife Priscilla; (because that Claudius had commanded all Jews to depart from Rome:) and came unto them. And because he was of the same craft, he abode with them, and wrought: for by their occupation they were tentmakers." (Acts 18:1-3)

"And a certain Jew named Apollos, born at Alexandria, an eloquent man, and mighty in the scriptures, came to Ephesus. This man was instructed in the way of the Lord; and being fervent in the spirit, he spoke

*and taught diligently the things of the Lord, knowing only
the baptism of John. And he began to speak boldly in the
synagogue: whom when Aquila and Priscilla had heard,
they took him unto them, and expounded unto him the way
of God more perfectly." (Acts 18:24-26)*

1. Peter's Wife (Matthew 8:14-18; Mark 1:29-34; Luke 4:38-41)

There are many powerful but unnamed wives in Scripture,
who remained in the background, supporting their husbands'
ministries.

a. What evidence is there that Peter had a wife? (Matthew 8:14)

b. Under what circumstances might Jesus have met Peter's
wife? (Matthew 8:15)

c. From an economic standpoint, describe the likely life-style
of Peter's wife. (Matthew 8:18-24)

d. What may Peter's wife have in common with modern
pastor's wives? (Acts 1:12-26)

e. At times, what did Peter's wife have in common with wives
of modern political prisoners? (Acts 12:1-9)

f. SUMMARY QUESTION: In what ways was Peter's wife
seemingly in the background, but probably a very powerful
influence on Peter's ministry? Compare and contrast their
marriage with that of Priscilla and Aquilla.

2. Abigail and Nabal (1 Samuel 25:1-42)

While Priscilla and Aquilla seem spiritually compatible,
Abigail and Nabal apparently were not. This forced Abigail
into a position of spiritual leadership within her family.

a. Economically and emotionally speaking, describe Abigail
and Nabal's marriage. (1 Samuel 25:2-3, 14-17, 25, 36)

b. What took place between Nabal and David? (25:4-10)

c. How was David about to respond to Nabal? (25:12-13, 21-22)

d. In what ways was Abigail's spiritual understanding at a higher level than that of her husband's? (25:26—31)

e. What type leadership role did Abigail play in her marriage, and what was the result of it? (25:18-35)

f. SUMMARY QUESTION: What are the differences and similarities between the marriages of Priscilla and Abigail? Discuss the two marriages in terms of the concepts of leadership and submission.

3. Deborah and Lapidoth (Judges 4—5)

Deborah seems to have had a more public leadership role than that of her husband.

a. Describe Deborah's role in Israel. (Judges 4:4-7)

b. What type of relationship did Deborah have with the men she led? (4:7-16; 5:1)

c. Compare and contrast the times in which Priscilla/Aquilla and Deborah/Lapidoth lived. (Acts 18:1-3; 24—26)

d. Compare and contrast Deborah and Priscilla in terms of the roles they seem to have played as wives.

e. Compare and contrast Lapidoth and Aquilla in terms of the roles they seem to have played as husbands.

f. SUMMARY QUESTION: What principles can be drawn from the marriages of Priscilla/Aquilla and Deborah/Lapidoth, and applied to marriages of working African Americans today?

4. Elisabeth and Zecharias (Luke 1:5-25, 57-68)

The extended family played an important role in Elisabeth and Zecharias' marriage. However, Elisabeth and Zecharias seemed to share the leadership within their family.

a. What problem did Elisabeth and Zecharias face, and what effect did it have on Elisabeth's view of herself? (Luke 1:6-7, 24-25)

b. Who was Elisabeth and Zecharias' extended family, what

53

did they have in common, and how did they support one another? (1:26-32, 31-43)

c. Compare and contrast Elisabeth and Zecharias' spiritual maturity. (1:6, 11-22, 24-25, 41-43, 57-67)

d. In what sense was Elisabeth similar to modern pastors's wives? (1:5-9)

e. Discuss the concepts of leadership and submission as it operated in Elisabeth and Zecharias' marriage. (Luke 1:5-25, 57-68)

f. SUMMARY QUESTION: Compare and contrast the marriage of Elisabeth/Zecharias with that of Priscilla/Aquilla. What principles can be drawn from their experiences, and applied to marriages between African American couples of today?

5. Joseph and Mary (Matthew 1:18-25)

Joseph assumed marital leadership in an unusual and potentially dangerous situation, while Mary seems to have remained in a very powerful leadership position within her family.

a. Explain the initial situation which required Joseph to assume leadership in a difficult situation. (Matthew 1:18-25)

b. What was another situation which required Joseph to assume leadership in a difficult situation? (Luke 2:1-7)

c. What was another situation which required Joseph to assume leadership in a difficult situation? (Matthew 2:11-15)

d. What is another way that Joseph assumed leadership? (Luke 2:41-52)

e. In what ways did the Lord speak to Mary and Joseph similarly? (Luke 1:26-35, 46-55; Matthew 1:18-25) Discuss the concepts of leadership and submission as it applies to their marriage.

f. SUMMARY QUESTION: Compare and contrast the marriages of Joseph/Mary and Aquilla/Priscilla. What, if any, principles can be drawn from these marriages and applied to African American marriages today?

6. FAMILY MINISTRY APPLICATION

Name some specific ways in which the family ministries of your church can develop programs which better meet the needs of a variety of two-parent family types.

7. PERSONAL APPLICATION

How might you classify various types of two-parent families and couples that exist within your extended family? If you are married, in what ways is your marriage similar or different from the biblical families studied in this chapter? Are there any principles that you can draw from them to apply to your situation?

CHAPTER THREE

SINGLE PARENT FAMILIES

"A severe malady does not always kill." (African proverb)

It was just minutes before the teacher's meeting of the volunteers for Vacation Bible School staff was to begin. Sister Elmore had just distributed the materials that would be used this year. As she glanced around the room, it suddenly occurred to her that there were no male volunteers this year.

Then she also realized that most of the women who had volunteered were single parents. Probably the oldest single parent was Mother Washington, whose husband had gone home to be with the Lord last October. A few other women were in similar circumstances. Two of the women were divorced from their husbands, having been victims of physical abuse and infidelity. Then there were several younger women in their early twenties, who had never been married, but who had several young elementary school age children.

As she prepared to begin the meeting, it also struck her that quite a large number of children who would attend VBS would be children whose fathers were not living with their families. In fact, some of the children who would attend probably had never met their fathers.

Sister Elmore wondered what this would mean in terms of her ministry to the teachers and the children.

This chapter focuses on the varieties of African American single parent families. It presents biblical principles for ministering to a variety of family types, and guidelines for ministering to single parent families. Problems facing single-parent families are explored, and the potential benefits of working through strong kinship bonds within the African American community are also explored.

The chapter is designed for people within families and within church communities who want to win, heal and equip single parent families for survival and service within the Community of Faith.

Varieties of Single Parent Families. Single parents are not a monolithic group. They are diverse. While the most common type of single parent is the one who became pregnant outside of marriage, a large number of single parents became parents as the result of incest or rape. We need to differentiate between these groups because they may have different needs for new learning and emotional healing.

Another type of single parent family is the one which results from the death of a spouse. The problems for the parent who remains with the children are those of loneliness, physical and emotional exhaustion, and often financial strain. Suddenly there is no partner to listen to those very private problems that the two parents used to discuss and resolve.

Yet another type of single parent family is the one which results from a divorce. One of the major problems that arises in such a situation is the need to juggle time in an attempt to function as two parents, and yet maintain some personal social life. There are also the inevitable difficulties of working out visiting hours and responsibilities with the absent parent.

The aftermath of divorce produces stages of guilt, self-incrimination, and hostility which need to be worked through. If one or both parties remarries, the family system becomes complex. New relationships have to be worked out. Instead of two adult personalities, there are now three or four people who must, to some degree, get along with each other.

For the children, divorce is not only the sudden loss of a parent, but also the loss of their day-to-day model who guides them in their development. While a model may not always have been a positive one, even a negative model can be missed, especially if the family's economic status goes down. An older child can identify the shortcomings of his parents and resolve to avoid them. However, the younger child cannot do this as easily as the older one. Most children of divorce spend at least the first year struggling with their own possible contribution to the divorce and daydreaming about the return of the missing parent.

While there are differences between single parent families, they also share many characteristics. For example, a large percentage have experienced poor living conditions, a lack of education and a lack of marketable work skills. If we were to form a hierarchy of families in America, based on their economic well-being from high to low, at the very bottom of the ladder would be the single, female-headed family. It seems that single mothers and their children are struggling most. According to the most recent statistics, at least one in every four African American children will be growing up in these circumstances.

Many of these children are required to take on too many responsibilities for self-care and that of younger sisters and brothers. Increasingly many of these single parents are young people who have little or no experience in parenting. The birth of their own baby at first may have been viewed as the arrival of someone to love them and to be loved. This short-lived experience may fade with the reality of day-to-day care giving without adequate help, funds or training.

Due to such discouraging circumstances, the single parent often abandons any view of the future or of actively working toward a goal. Offering ongoing motivation and hope is a vital part of all ministries to single parents.

When ministering to the single parent, the church, family and counselor must help her deal with standard problems such as the need to become economically independent, the need for housing, the need to network for support, the need for wholeness and the need to cope with sexual desire. Systematic training in parenting should begin even before the birth of the baby and be available thereafter. Along with all of the above the young single parent needs continued nurturing into maturity. Many are young adolescents themselves who have lost an important part of growing into adulthood.

The Need for Independence. One form of ministry to single parents is helping them become economically independent. This along with value training and a committed life can help break the cycle of repeated unwed pregnancies. We must consider the fact that we truly help people when we teach them how to fish, not when we just give them fish. If we are going to help build self-confidence and self-esteem, we must help people become increasingly more empowered and more in charge of their lives.

To be in a chronically dependent state is to be in a chronic state of childhood, with all of the resulting characteristics of being helpless, child-like and giving up responsibility for one's self. Helping them achieve independence, of course, means helping the single parent locate job training, so that s/he can acquire marketable skills. Assisting the single parent to remain or return to school is essential. Current information on career choices, available educational resources, GED preparation and literacy programs should be available in the church or on the church's referral list.

The Need for Suitable Housing. A second focus of our ministry should be on housing. Many single parents have experienced discrimination in obtaining housing. A very good project for individual churches or collectives of churches would be to purchase apartment buildings and use them for housing single parents.

These houses could be modeled along the lines of those that have been constructed for senior citizens. We could incorporate day care within the apartment building and could begin shaping the educational and spiritual development of the children at very early ages. We know more about human personality now. We realize that we cannot begin too early in life to develop healthy personalities.

We know that there are prenatal influences such as drug abuse and nutrition which shape babies even before they are born. The earlier we begin our ministry with these mothers, the better. The crucial first five years are so important. We begin to see developmental lags in our young Black children from under-nourished homes that are expressed as early as two and three years of age. Until apartments can be purchased or built, how effective it would be to have a selection of Christian homes which would take in single parents and their children. Perhaps matching some of them with career singles or senior citizens would enrich both sets of lives if the church offers guidelines and support.

The Need for Wholeness. The third focus of our ministry should be providing the framework within which single parent families can feel complete or whole. The concept of the extended family has to be developed in the church so that when a father is absent, the father image can still exist for the children. Through the extended church family network, when the mother is missing, the mother image can still exist for the children. In both cases, the remaining parents can find support among other believers.

The congregation can be divided into smaller cross-generational groups which include males and females, intact families, single families and singles to function as extended families to one another, based not on genetics but on spiritual values.

The ministry of the church must be directed to the whole family system and this must begin as early as possible. Such a ministry is not restricted to a one- to three-hour program. The more we can develop a ministry that encompasses a greater portion of the single parent's life, the more we can offer the extended family concept. Ongoing support is the greatest need of single parents whose time for self is usually not available. Often someone to take the children to the doctor or the library or skating offers the needed break that can minimize abuse and offer relief.

61

We must ask ourselves certain questions. One is whether we as individuals are attempting to minister to single families, or whether we are a part of a church that is doing so. Another is how we can maximize the support we can offer to an individual, to his/her children, to the family and to the grandmothers involved who often are the day-to-day care givers. We have to examine the whole family system and determine what we can do to support each part of that system.

The Need to Network. The fifth focus of our ministry with the single parent must be on developing a network of supportive help to assist in taking care of the children. One source of support is the missing parent. In spite of adults' personal attitudes, the children should be helped to maintain respect and contact with the missing parent, if possible. Whether the absence of the parent is caused by death or separation, the children must be helped to work through the resulting stages of emotions (such as grief and loss) with helpful friends and/or competent professionals.

Networking involves forming friendships with persons in similar situations as well as with intact families. This is important for the parent, as well as for the children. Both can use this period of life for growth, independence, expansion of personality and development of mind. During this period, single parents can become a part of an intimate and warm fellowship of Christians that is responsive to their needs.

The Need to Cope with Sexuality. Most single parents will experience some conflict in the area of their personal sexuality. This is quite a problem for younger single parents, in particular. Those who have been in long-term or short-term sexual relationships have awakened these drives. Many are convinced that this is the way to hold a man. Men make heavy demands on women to comply on their terms since men are in short supply. The Bible forbids any Christian from being involved in adultery or fornication. However, many single parents have been sexually active since they were 11 or 12 years of age.

They have experienced sexual behavior, if not intense sexual drives. Many have strong sexual drives, intensified by their need for love, attention and belonging. Many have felt that, by having sex, they could temporarily meet some of these basic needs. Moreover, television and the secular world promote the use of the attractiveness of one's body to get attention and approval. Therefore, they use their bodies and sexual experiences as a means of fulfilling their emotional needs.

The problem for them, however, is that even when they do use their bodies in this way, the sexual experience itself may be completely unsatisfying to them. It is unsatisfying because, as females, they want ongoing emotional commitment and caring, not just a fly-by-night physical or biological experience. That is why so many single parents find themselves in real dilemmas, as far as sexuality is concerned. In addition in today's world there is the real threat of disease and/or death as a result of unsafe sex.

What is even more disheartening is that, in the course of trying to meet their needs in this unsatisfying way, they often get straddled with the responsibility of children. Very often, the spin off is that they must bear the burden alone of rearing the children. They must cope with this dilemma after losing an intense though short-term relationship. They may have gotten pregnant after a one-night stand. They may have been a novice, sexually. They were not necessarily promiscuous. It may be that they just didn't protect themselves.

In any case, this single parent must work through the grief of the loss of a mate, or potential mate, while assuming the role of a caretaker of their children.

Most churches do not help single parents in these areas. Churches rarely share with them or teach them that the sex drive has to be acknowledged. It is a drive that can go unmet and not damage them, physically. However, it is a reality. The church needs to teach them that there are ways of dealing with sexual desire that minimize its effect other than going out and disobeying God.

We need to use plain talk that mothers and grandmothers used to use. We just need to go ahead and tell them, "Keep your dress down! Go take a cold shower. Run around the block every night." There is an urgent need for this because we have so many children having children. They don't have the wisdom of knowing how to parent.

Some of that good common sense that helped past generations avoid mistakes is missing for them. Young people today don't hear the information they need at school. Therefore, they get caught up in peer group pressure and their own sexual drives. The result is that they don't know how to handle it all.

We must teach them the signals and signs of danger, because they know so little about sex. They think they do, but they don't. Many have allowed matters to progress to the point where they have lost control. They need Christians to help them identify the early signals of danger. For example, they need to be told not to go to someone's house unless an adult is there.

Many of them don't know how to date. They don't know how to plan activities. Often two young people come together and become so relaxed that they just end up getting involved physically. They don't realize that there are activities other than sex.

Talking to them is not enough. In youth meetings and other places where they are gathered, we need to engage them in actual role playing and dramas which give them the opportunity to practice appropriate behaviors. For example, role playing might provide them with the opportunity to answer questions such as: When you're out on a date and the boy wants physical intimacy, what can you do to change the situation around? How should you plan your dates to try to prevent them from ending up in the back seat of a car? What do you say to preserve your dignity and adhere to your standards without emasculating the other person?

Through role playing and drama, we can provide them with the words, and allow them to try them out. Through these activities, they can develop skills of behaving in the correct way. Actual group recreation, sports and travel can be planned for them. Young people need to be kept busy in worthwhile activities. Church should be open every evening and weekends for them.

In dealing with this issue, we are often countering cultural resistance against new ways of looking at sexuality. For example, we have some traditions and some history that we as African Americans must face. This history has had an effect on our view of sexuality. That is, the definition of manhood, in the past, often related to sexual performance. Boys and men must be taught responsibility and accountability early on in this area. Training for manhood is a necessity. Moreover, we also defined womanhood in terms of whether someone was a mother. Becoming a mother made a girl become an adult, or mature, in other words.

This has caused our young girls to believe that, once they become mothers, they can be treated with more respect within the family. In fact, often the young women feel that, once they have a baby, they will be allowed to move out from under the authority of the parent. With a child, they think, they will no longer be considered a child. Many young women also feel that they must prove their femininity by having a baby.

Another part of our slave history which sometimes shapes our view of sexuality is that sexual activity was always free and available to Black people, when, in other areas of life, they were in bondage. Sex was not controlled by the larger society as it was in our preslave history in Africa. With these types of beliefs still governing the sexual attitudes of our young people, there is a need for systematic Christian teachings in this area.

The Need to Cope with the Death of a Spouse. When the single parent is single due to the death of a spouse, the counselor, church and family will need to help the remaining partner move through the grieving process. Interestingly enough, children are affected less by death of a spouse than by the divorce of a spouse. They can accept death because they don't feel responsible. However, in divorce, they often feel responsible and they don't handle it quite as well. Discussion groups for children of divorced parents may be useful. Acknowledgement of their feelings and Sunday School lessons without the individual children being pointed out can be validating.

The Need for Self-Esteem. Families, churches and counselors of single parents must be concerned about helping them develop wholesome self-esteem. They are not going to develop it just by our telling them how great they are. Although it is important, just telling them is a mere beginning. We need to design situations and create opportunities for them to perform in the ways that we know they can do well. Then we need to help them see themselves in this new light, drawing their own conclusions about themselves.

These are the types of situations that are substantive and real, not just artificially contrived. We need to provide them with experiences that develop good feelings for them from the inside out, as a consequence of having the concrete experiences in which they see themselves and know that they are capable and growing. These types of situations can begin a process of healing for single parents who have experienced so much discouragement in other areas of their lives.

Single parent families are generally born of crisis and disorganization. They need help in recovering through reorganization and stabilization. They remain vulnerable to physical and emotional demands which result in high levels of stress. The single parent as the head of the household needs to learn management skills and the creative use of resources. Vacation Bible School classes could collect coupons for giving. Adult Sunday School class, B.T.U. groups and missionary circles could have Mother's Day outings on Saturday afternoons and provide activities for children at the church. Intact families, couples or singles could "adopt" a single family for holidays.

Summary. This chapter has focused on varieties of single parent families. It has presented principles for ministering to single parent families, outlining typical problems they must face, and ways of helping them overcome these problems. The following exercise provides the opportunity to apply principles presented in this chapter to the study of a biblical family.

BIBLE FAMILIES

INSTRUCTIONS: The Bible contains the stories of many single parent families. The following exercise allows you to study some of these families. The first five exercises consist of "fill-in-the-blank" questions, followed by a summary question. The sixth exercise allows you to apply the wisdom you gained from this chapter to the development of a family ministry in your local church. The seventh exercise allows you to make personal applications.

The Widow and Her Son

"Now when he came nigh to the gate of the city, behold, there was a dead man carried out, the only son of his mother, and she was a widow: and much people of the city was with her. And when the Lord saw her, he had compassion on her, and said unto her, Weep not. And he came and touched the bier: and they that bare him stood still. And he said, Young man, I say unto thee, Arise. And he that was dead sat up and began to speak. And he delivered him to his mother."
(Luke 7:12-15)

1. Eunice (Acts 16:1-3; 2 Timothy 1:5; 3:14, 15; 4:5)

In Scripture, Eunice is usually presented alone without the name of the father of her son. For a time, at least, Eunice probably was a single parent.

a. Who was Eunice's son, and what type influence did she have on his life? (Acts 16:1-3; 2 Timothy 1:5; 3:15)

67

b. What influence did the extended family have on Eunice and Timothy? (2 Timothy 1:5)

c. What role did Timothy have in the Community of Faith? (Acts 16:3; 1 Timothy 1:18-19; 4:14; 2 Timothy 4:5)

d. How might Timothy's early teachings from Eunice have shaped his later personality? (Philippians 2:19-22)

e. How might early training have prepared him for his role in the life of the Apostle Paul? (Acts 16:2; 17:14; 19:22; Philippians 1:1; 2:19; Colossians 1:1; Philemon 1)

f. SUMMARY QUESTION: What messages are sent to single parents from the above passages?

2. Hagar (Genesis 16; 21:9-17; 25:12; Galatians 4:24, 25)

Hagar had a very difficult time as a single parent.

a. How did Hagar become a parent? (Genesis 16)

b. What problems developed for Hagar in the household of Abraham and Sarah? (16:4-6)

c. How did Hagar come to know the Lord? (16:4-16)

d. What conflicts developed between Hagar and Sarah once Hagar returned to Sarah's household? (21:1-13)

e. How did Hagar become a single parent, and how did she raise her son? (21:14-21)

f. SUMMARY QUESTION: What messages are being sent to single parents from the above passages?

3. Mary, Mother of James and Joses (Matthew 27:55-61; Mark 15:40, 47; 16:1; Luke 24:10)

Mary always appears alone with her sons in Scripture. She probably raised them alone.

a. Who was part of Mary's extended family? (Matthew 27:56; Mark 15:40; Luke 24:10)

b. Where was Mary at the crucifixion of Christ? (Matthew 27:30-56, 58-61; Mark 15:40)

c. What role did she play at the time of the resurrection of Christ? (Mark 16:1, 8)

d. Who were James' brothers? (Matthew 27:56; Luke 6:16)

e. What role did James eventually play in the Community of Faith? (Matthew 10:1-5; Mark 3:18; Luke 6:15; Acts 1:13)

f. SUMMARY QUESTION: What messages are being sent to single parents from the above passages?

4. Tamar (Genesis 38:6-30; 1 Chronicles 2:4; Matthew 1:3)

The Lord overlooked Tamar's faults and saw her need.

a. What happened to Tamar's first marriage? (Genesis 38:2-7; Numbers 26:19)

b. What happened to Tamar's second marriage? (Genesis 38:6-10)

c. How did Tamar eventually have sons? (Genesis 38:11-30)

d. How did the Lord eventually use Tamar's life? (Matthew 1:3)

e. What does Tamar's life say about the ability of the Lord to turn a bad situation around? (Ruth 4:12; Matthew 3:1; Genesis 38:27-30; 1 Chronicles 2:4; 9:4; 11:11; 27:2; Nehemiah 11:4-6)

f. SUMMARY QUESTION: What messages are being sent to single parents from the above passages?

5. Pharaoh's Daughter (Exodus 2:5-10; Acts 7:21; Hebrews 11:24)

Today there are a growing number of single women who are adopting children, as single parents.

a. What was the environment of oppression in which Pharaoh's daughter lived? (Exodus 1:8-22)

b. How did Pharaoh's daughter encounter the child she adopted? (2:1-6)

c. Who were the members of Moses' "extended family," and what impact did they have on his life? (2:7-11)

d. Indirectly, what major impact did Pharaoh's daughter have on the Children of Israel as a group? (3:1-10)

e. Compare and contrast Pharaoh's daughter with the widow of Luke 7:11-15.

f. SUMMARY QUESTION: What messages are being sent to single parents from the above passages?

6. FAMILY MINISTRY APPLICATION

What specific ways can your church improve its ministry to single parents?

7. PERSONAL APPLICATION

Are there single parents within your extended family network? How do the above exercises apply to these families?

CHAPTER FOUR

HUSBANDS AND WIVES GROWING

"Compare thing with thing, compare matter with matter and then forgive (the matter) that thou mayest be praised." (African Proverb)

Mr. and Mrs. Cunningham signed up for counseling. Mr. Cunningham complained, saying that lately his wife had changed. She wasn't like she always had been. Before, all she thought about was him and the children. Now she was talking about going back to work and pursuing the career she abandoned when she first started having children. She said she was bored at home, and now that the children were in high school, she wanted to pursue some of her personal interests. She said she wanted to start teaching again, and during the summers pursue her master's degree. Mr. Cunningham was a "self-made-man" who had dropped out of high school, but had taken up a trade and been quite successful.

During the course of the counseling sessions, it surfaced that Mrs. Cunningham's potential independence always had been an issue between them, but they had avoided discussing it while the children where growing up. Over the years, Mrs. Cunningham had tried to become involved with various Christian Education ministries at church, hoping that this would provide her with some intellectual stimulation, but her hus-

band had always stopped her, saying that it would take her away from him and the children.

She had been teaching when they got married, but she stopped because her husband said he wanted to have children. He seemed to enjoy telling his friends that he had taken her away from her career as a teacher. Recently, Mrs. Cunningham had become more assertive. This had led to arguments which were becoming more and more emotional. Mrs. Cunningham feared that her new desire for independence would threaten her marriage.

It is not uncommon for couples to change over the course of married life. However, often changes in one partner or the other can be the source of conflict within the marriage, with one of the spouses feeling that the other spouse has somehow violated the basic marriage contract. Couples in conflict may approach counselors for help.

This chapter focuses on how Christian counselors and others can help a couple grow, rather than drift apart, as a result of natural developmental changes within one spouse or the other and related differences of opinion. When counseling couples in conflict, some issues are fairly general and affect couples whether they are Black, white, or brown.

Then there is another set of issues which seem of particular concern to African American families. Counseling couples in conflict involves starting where each person is, and assisting them in identifying and resolving issues, gaining new insights, attitudes, values, beliefs, behaviors, commitments and resources for abundant living. The chapter explores the nature of the counseling process, and provides guidelines for dealing with specific types of conflicts that can occur in marriage.

What Non-professional Counseling Is. Counseling is relational helping. It usually occurs over time and requires developing a helping relationship. The term relationship carries with it certain implications. Counseling is not merely handing out advice. On the contrary, counseling requires an investment of self, energy and time. Counseling requires developing a unique type of relationship. The uniqueness of it is important. It differs from other relationships that we have since it is for the sole benefit of the other person. Counseling is one of the hardest jobs we can do because the way we interact with a person in counseling is foreign to the way we normally interact.

Counseling and Confidentiality. Counseling requires developing a relationship which permits trust. If I enter into a counseling relationship, I invite you to be open with me. I also promise to be confidential. Most people have not learned how to be confidential. The inability to keep secrets has caused havoc within Christian circles.

We are not going to have people being very open with us for very long in a closed setting if we have not learned to honor their openness by learning to keep what they tell us private and confidential. Neither are we going to get people to be open with us if our first response to honest and true feelings is to "pounce" on the person who expresses them and/or judge them. If we do this in counseling, we will stop them from telling us anything else.

Openness says, "I'm inviting you to tell me how you really feel." All people long for openness. We don't often experience it because often if we honestly share, a person may judge us and hold the feelings against us. We fear that they are always going to see us in the light of how we felt at that particular time, and subsequently they will not allow for growth in our lives.

Counseling, Introspection, and Self-Worth. Counseling is a unique type of relationship that facilitates introspection. In other words, a counselor wants to set up a relationship with a counselee that will encourage him/her to look inside of him/herself. An individual can only do this if the counselor accepts the person unconditionally.

A counselee should not have to go through the usual game playing to convince the counselor of the counselee's value and worth. The counselee shouldn't have to convince the counselor that s/he is valuable, smart and can take care of him/herself. The counselee needs to be free to put all of those games to rest. The counselor must create the type of environment that conveys the idea that the counselor is convinced of the value of human beings. Some of us may not be. We may be convinced of the value of a Christian, but we may not be convinced of the value of the human being who doesn't know the Lord. We have to be convinced of the value of that human being also, regardless of a person's past or present dilemma.

God was convinced of that. He was so convinced, He was willing to send His Son for unredeemed man. Therefore we need to be convinced that there is value in every human being—even in the person at the lowest rung of the ladder, who may be caught up in all kinds of problems, depressions and negativism. The person in this state is also a human being for whom God sent His Son. God loves him. Before the counselor or counselee could respond to or return the love of God, God loved him/her.

Only if the counselor is likewise convinced of the value of human beings can s/he really create an environment that fosters openness for counselees. Counselees can feel this environment. They know it. They hear it in what you say and they see it in the counselor's body language. They recognize discrepancies between verbal and non-verbal expressions.

The Spiritual Dimension of Counseling. Counseling is not one person solving another person's problems. It is a collaborative relationship. The wounded, the Healer and the counselor collaborate. As Christians, we are the third party that collaborates in the triad (Counselor, Counselee and God). The triad works to bring about new perspectives, new thinking, new attitudes, new beliefs, and new behavior.

All of these go together. Thinking and behavior have to go together. What we are trying to do in our counseling is to promote Christian maturity. We want to develop an inward character which conforms to the character of Christ. It means facilitating an encounter between the person and God around the identified issue or problem. Using the Word of God appropriately is a skill to be learned by Christians.

After becoming saved through a personal relationship with Christ, the process of taking on the character of Christ begins from the inside out. This means a reexamination of our attitudes, our intents, our motivations, our purposes, and our behaviors. Romans 12 states a principle of transformation through the renewing of our mind. Another part of discipling is learning to react to problem circumstances in a manner that's consistent with the life of God within us. This is very practical.

It becomes real in terms of everyday crises in everyday life. This linking up into God and accessing His power is what happens when we experience loss, success, abandonment, death, separation and things not going our way. We respond differently when people don't recognize us or respond to us in the wrong way. This is the goal that we have in mind for the people we counsel.

Another outcome is that they will be better equipped to deal with conflicts that surface during the normal course of married life. To prepare to help a hurting family, begin by going through the Gospel and studying Jesus, the Counselor. The Books of Matthew, Mark, Luke, and John feature numerous instances where Jesus is seen counseling people. In studying these passages we need to identify the techniques He used. The Lord used a large repertoire of counseling techniques. "Confrontation" and "problem management" are two techniques that can be used.

Confrontation in Counseling. There is a role for confrontation in counseling after establishing a relationship. If you are a change agent, there are times when confrontation has to occur. However, if we begin with confrontation we're going to lose or antagonize most people. Therefore we must begin our counseling by showing that we care, and this takes varying lengths of time. It requires time to discover how the counselee sees his life situation. This is through attentive listening. Once we know this, we can gradually begin to confront a counselee about specific issues.

For example, the Samaritan woman, whom Jesus counseled, had been caught in adultery. This is an excellent passage for illustrating the principle of caring before confrontation. Jesus allows her to sense His support before she suspects that He may criticize her behavior. This story is a good model for helping clients deal with criticism.

A floor of affirmation must undergird assertiveness. A gift of understanding opens the way to disagreeing. An awareness of love makes us free to level with one another. We must present the same message, but repeat it a number of different ways. For example, when we are counseling young people from troubled families, we often make the mistake of criticizing certain of their behaviors right away.

However, we must remember that young people are people who are at a different stage in a process of transformation. They may do things that we feel are incorrect or are indeed wrong based on the Bible and not just tradition. Because of this, often our first response is to criticize. However, Jesus shows, in the conversation with the Samaritan woman, that empathy must precede evaluation. A basis of trust must be laid before advice can be given.

Setting Goals and Rewarding Accomplishments. Counselors need to set up concrete goals and ways that the counselee can know when some of these goals have been achieved. When they are achieved, celebrations are in order. When the counselee doesn't "blow up", you can celebrate together. You can celebrate when they exercise real love in an unloving situation. The celebrations can take many forms—dinner out for a couple, good books, or relief from ironing.

Perhaps it is the inner satisfaction of the counselee knowing that she has made one more step in becoming more like the

Lord. We need to relish these moments and enjoy them. These celebrations help them proceed to the next accomplishment, and take the next step. All of the attitudes and techniques are useful for couples to use with each other as well as between the counselor and client. Listed below is a process that has many applications in male/female relationships. It is a problem management model with four major phases:

Relationship Building. This is the phase in which a willingness to listen to another person's point of view is important. During this phase, permission to express feelings without fear of attack or judgment is given, along with openness to exploring one's own feelings and sharing of perceptions of what is happening. This phase generally requires learning for men who need to factor feelings and emotions into a problem. It leads to recognition of the issues and problems.

Problem Exploration and Clarification. During this phase, together, the husband/wife/counselor are allowed to state and understand what the problems are. A search for insights, information and resources begins.

Problem Solutions. The counselor should help the client reformulate or restate the solution to the problem from a spiritual perspective. Scriptures (such as Romans 12) can be used here to restate the solution in scriptural terms. The Lord also uses human beings (both professional and non-professional) and technological resources. Solutions may involve a weekly evening together for a couple for fun and relaxation.

It may include the sharing of a dishwashing task. Reordering the budget, returning to school, beginning a family Bible study, goal setting and other ideas can be included in a package of proposed solutions. Creative brainstorming is very helpful along with knowledge of available alternatives and resources. Periodically reviewing progress and reworking solutions is generally important.

Most couples enter marriage with unrealistic expectations. They desperately hope it will be the fulfillment of their dreams and the solution to their hurts and ills. Much of couple counseling is an uncovering of hurts and replacing them by considering realistic new expectations from humans and accepting complete fulfillment only in Christ.

Action Plan Review. Resources and supports are usually needed to encourage couples to continue working at new behavior. Periodically they should review their program for change, revise their objectives and establish new goals.

Conflicts Over the Roles of Women. Today Black women are benefiting from educational opportunities which open other opportunities to them. Many have very responsible positions and earn as much or more than the average male. This has allowed many to become more independent than they have ever been before. However parents are still raising girls who have the dream of marrying and becoming parents themselves.

It is important to understand that financial independence does not kill the desire for intimacy in most professional Black women. Even though some say they do not want marriage, and many even say they don't want relationships, most really do. Statements to the contrary are often a reaction to the bad experiences that they have had with Black men. Often these bad experiences can be traced to unrealistic expectations, differences in sex role socialization or men taking advantage of women.

Variations of problems exist for professional Black women whether they are married or single. Many young college women have had disappointments with young college men they have dated. These young women cannot understand it when the young men retreat from a relationship and protect themselves by saying, "I don't need you, I can make it by myself," after initiating contact with them.

When many of these same women enter the business world and are successful, they find that they are not always completely happy inside. In fact, they are very lonely since most social life is designed for couples. It's one thing to make a middle-income salary, be able to have your own apartment and contribute to your family. However, most women who can do this still have

78

the need to depend and to be linked intimately with a mate.

However, they don't want to become slaves. When they say they aren't interested in marriage, they mean that they don't want what their mothers have had to endure. Many consider what their mothers endured as abuse. They saw their mothers as "hanging in there" but not happy. Most of these women want to be treated as equals within marriage, using their education and gifts to make the home work more efficiently.

The protective defenses of women who have experienced financial independence and success, often say, "I don't need you (men) to protect me from being hurt, or from being let down." However, what is still most important to them is their family. If they put their relationships in a hierarchy, family relationships would be at the top of it. As counselors, we must help professional Black women admit their needs, carefully select potential mates and learn how to help them become all that they are capable of becoming.

This may require them to examine their values and recognize that degrees and annual incomes are not the measure of a man. Upwardly mobile professional males may have little time for much else. Women and men need to be able to say, "I want to be respected and you want to be respected. In order to get that respect for myself, we must learn how to show respect for one another." That's where counselors must begin working with both young women and young men. We've got to get them to cut through the ridiculous games that prevent them from meeting one another's needs. Each experiences enough stress from the world through societal factors.

Lower-income women in particular discuss the abuse some have experienced in relationships. This abuse is both physical and psychological. It is difficult to experience humiliation in the outside world and then return home to find it awaiting you there as well. This applies to men as well. Family ministry will equip couples through planning low cost couples' retreats and renewal workshops. Given the crisis in African American marriages, perhaps churches should rethink their organizational structures and offer more opportunities for couples to learn to work and play together.

Conflicts Resulting from Childhood Socialization. Differences exist between the socialization of women, and these differences can lead to conflict within any couple, regardless of race. For example, men have been reared and socialized to see the world differently than women. Think about the way a boy is raised in this society. Our society begins perceiving him differently than the girl, even before he is born. Mothers and fathers don't handle boys the same way that they handle girls.

When we toss boy children into the air, we toss the boys up higher than we do the girls, and a little rougher. We prepare them for risk taking. We automatically assume that we need to prepare them for the world. They are not encouraged to accept and express feelings as reality. We assume that they need tough skin. Parents encourage young men to develop a style of communication that is more direct and usually less intuitive.

These basic differences in approaches to girls and boys are the root causes of many conflicts that develop later, within their marriages.

Conflicts Between Parents and Sons Concerning Parenting. Fathers treat their sons differently than they treat their girls. Often fathers do not develop close or intimate relationships with their sons, but their interactions occur around issues of gender expectation and preparation. During adolescence it is not uncommon for the father to become alienated from the son, resenting/fearing the existence of another man in the household. This can lead to conflicts between father and son.

The father's fear is parallel to the fears a woman often has of accepting another woman in the household, even when the woman is her own daughter. During adolescence, conflicts also develop between mothers and sons, and these conflicts can surface again, in the son's later marriage. These mother/son conflicts can be traced to the fact that the boy child was reared primarily by the mother, on a day-to-day basis. However, at adolescence, he considers himself in the process of becoming a man.

In his view, part of that process involves separating from the mother, so that he can be different. Part of becoming a man is to guard against intimacy, control emotional openness and avoid the giving of himself. Therefore the adolescent boy feels compelled to think differently and solve problems differently than his mother would solve them. He becomes very concerned about showing that he is a man and mom is a woman. This means he asserts that he sees things differently than his mother.

On the other hand the girl becomes a woman by identifying with her mother. She becomes like a mother, in that nurturing becomes important to her if she has had a nuturing mother. There are differences between men and women in that more men seek independence and autonomy, whereas more women seek emotional intimacy, as important goals in adulthood. Now everything is fine until we bring the two of these people, raised so differently, together in marriage.

The differences surface immediately when men and women from marriages in conflict come to the counselor. Often the woman begins by saying, "I want him to talk to me. I want him to open up and share his private thoughts and self. I don't want him to keep that part of himself closed off. I want to be able to do that with him. I want us to really share in this area."

Then when their husbands come in, they say, "She knows I love her. I take care of her. She wants me to talk, but I can't do this. That's just not me. I can't do that. She wants something from me that I can't give, so I feel uncomfortable. I feel like she's possessing me. I am trapped, and I don't like it. She scares me a little bit when she starts demanding closeness and I have to sort of keep my distance in order to maintain control."

Often when the men perceive that they are getting too close, they do something to back away, to get some distance. The woman will not know why he is doing it, neither will the man. He won't know why he reacted with irritability or aloofness.

Often men feel that if they are too tender they won't be masculine. They think tenderness might make them lose control and be taken advantage of by a wife. Many feel that if they have to deal with internal thoughts and conflicts, they might uncover something that will make them seem like a dependent child.

It can become very confusing for men sometimes. It appears, in some cases, there may be a predisposition in them toward this type of thinking. In other cases, it appears to be a learned behavior related to our society. These types of conflicts also surface when a man is asked to express a need he may have. He may have difficulty doing this because he has been raised to feel that he must be all sufficient, because someone must depend on him. When those who have been raised to feel responsible and are unable due to obstacles to succeed in their roles, they experience deep depression and withdrawal. Therefore, when the man really does have great needs, but cannot express them, this constitutes a serious problem in marriage.

Conflicts Over the Internal Parent/Child. Three parts of us interact with other people to bring about healthy relationships. These are parent, adult and child. Parents dominate sometimes, but they also care and they nurture. They discipline. These are the authorities we know, and when it comes down to the bottom line, they are controlling. When we think about how adults function, we think of them as:

- dependable
- goal oriented
- realistic planners
- thoughtful
- logical
- capable of cooperation and mutuality
- capable of giving and receiving

Another part of us is the child. Most of us can name characteristics of children. We think of them as:

- self-centered
- free
- spontaneous

Eric Berne says that, within each of us, there are all three ways of interacting with others. In one-on-one group relationships, we relate to people for whom we are responsible based on whether we are being an adult parent or a child. In marriages one person sometimes becomes a parent and the other becomes the child. Most parents cannot be happy with anyone else but a child. A parent needs a child. A child needs a parent. So, in the marriage there is a male and a female. In some marriages, the male becomes the parent. (It's reversed in others.)

In such marriages, the question becomes: How does a parent man interact with a child woman? What would life be like? In a family like this, how are conflicts resolved? If the man is the parent, his primary way of relating to the woman would be that of telling the woman, not listening. He would also feel that he possesses the woman: "I own you. I have the right to tell you what to do."

Now the more the parent man sees the female as a child, the more he sees himself as the big daddy or big parent. This means that he could be a very caring and nurturing father. For a while this may work, because that may be what the woman perceives she needs at a given time.

However, what happens if after five, ten or fifteen years of marriage, she grows up? Then she may not want a daddy anymore. She may then resent what she initially accepted, the very thing that attracted her to the man. That's what often happens in male/female relationships. Sometimes the very thing that attracts becomes the source of conflict. Sometimes one person undergoes change while another person doesn't.

It may also happen in the reverse. The parent may be the female and the child the male. The man wants a mother. He thinks he needs someone to take care of him. He thinks he needs someone to be responsible, someone who looks out for him and plans for him.

What causes conflict is that people have these needs, but they don't know how to get them fulfilled in their marriages. This is all the more difficult if there has been a history of previous pain in that area of their lives. Ideally husbands and wives, wherever they find themselves interacting at this point in time will seek to find ways of fulfilling their needs that encourage each to keep growing.

Interacting sometimes requires allowing the child within each of them to meet, play and romance while, at other times, interacting involves nurturing and protecting one another as parents. Interacting means calling upon one another to value the relationship so highly that both try to make it work for them.

Summary. This chapter has presented an overview of the counseling process, as it relates to helping couples grow, rather than separate, as a result of differences. It explores a variety of conflicts in marriages, many of which can be traced to differences in child rearing and socialization between men and women. These conflicts include those between parents over how to handle children and internal parent/child/adult conflicts, and how to handle typical conflicts of Black women. The chapter also presented guidelines for counseling families that are experiencing some of these conflicts, and which also may be useful for couples wanting to improve their marriages.

The following exercise provides an opportunity to apply some of the principles presented in this chapter to conflicts faced by a biblical family.

BIBLE FAMILIES

INSTRUCTIONS: The following exercises allow you to examine biblical couples who struggled, in their marriages, over time, as they grew. The first five exercises consist of "fill-in-the- blank" questions, followed by a summary question. The sixth exercise allows you to apply the wisdom you gained from this chapter to the development of a family ministry in your local church. The seventh exercise allows you to make personal applications.

Abraham and Sarah

"And he said, Men, brethren, and fathers, hearken; The God of glory appeared unto our father Abraham, when he was in Mesopotamia, before he dwelt in Charran, And said unto him, Get thee out of thy country, and from thy kindred, and come into the land which I shall show thee. Then came he out of the land of the Chaldeans, and dwelt in Charran: and from thence, when his father was dead, he removed him into this land, wherein ye now dwell.

"And he gave him none inheritance in it, no, not so much as to set his foot on; yet he promised that he would give it to him for a possession, and to his seed after him, when as yet he had no child. And God spake on this wise, That his seed should sojourn in a strange land; and that they should bring them into bondage, and entreat them evil four hundred years.

"And the nation to whom they shall be in bondage will I judge, said God: and after that shall they come forth, and serve me in this place. And he gave him the covenant of circumcision: and so Abraham begat Isaac, and circumcised him the eighth day; and Isaac begat Jacob; and Jacob begat the twelve patriarchs." (Acts 7:2-8)

1. Abraham's Call (Genesis 11:27-31; 12:1-9, 11-20; Hebrews 12:8-10, 11-20, 27-31)

During the early years, following Abraham's initial call, conditions surrounding married life must have been quite unpredictable.

a. Imagine and describe what married life may have been like for Sarah, and then for Abraham, during the early years of their marriage. (Genesis 11:27-31)

b. Imagine and describe what married life may have been like for Sarah, and then for Abraham, during the years immediately following his call. (12:1-9)

c. What might Abraham and Sarah have learned from their ordeal in Egypt, and how might this have affected their marriage? (12:11-20)

d. Why did Abraham travel so much? (Hebrews 11:8-10)

e. Explain some of the apparent contradictions in Abraham's spiritual life, and how this could have affected his marriage. (11:27-31; 12:11-20)

f. SUMMARY QUESTION: If you were to classify the way in which Abraham and Sarah related to one another during this period, which one is behaving as the "adult," "parent" or "child?"

2. Separation from Lot (Genesis 11:25-32; 12:1, 4, 5; 13:1-13)

Up until the separation from Lot, Abraham's original extended family still played a role in his married life.

a. Who was Lot, and how did he come to live with Abraham and Sarah? (Genesis 11:25-32; 12:1, 4-5)

b. Describe life in the extended family of Abraham, Sarah, and Lot, once Abraham left Egypt. (13:1-5)

c. What family conflicts developed between Lot and Abraham, and what dangers might this have imposed on the well-being of the family? (13:6-7)

d. How was the problem between Lot and Abraham resolved? (13:8-12)

e. Summarize some of the changes that took place in the marriage of Sarah and Abraham, and in the role of the extended family. (13:1-13)

f. SUMMARY QUESTION: Can any parallels be drawn between Abraham and Sarah's extended family and African American extended families today? What spiritual principles can be learned from this story?

3. The Need for an Heir (Hebrews 11:8-10; Genesis 12:11-17; 15:1-7, 18-21; 16:1-6)

During this phase of Abraham and Sarah's marriage, Sarah becomes more visible.

a. How did Abraham contradict himself when it came to trusting God? (Hebrews 11:8-10; Genesis 15:1-3)

b. What were some of God's promises to Abraham? (15:4-7, 18-21)

c. Sarah is somewhat less quiet than she had been in earlier stages of her marriage to Abraham. Describe this change. (12:11-17; 16:1-3)

d. Why was Abraham so eager to follow Sarah's suggestion? (15:1-3; 16:1-4)

e. What problems did the conception of Hagar (the surrogate mother) cause for the Abraham/Sarah household? (16:4-6)

f. SUMMARY QUESTION: If you were to classify Sarah and Abraham in the way they related to one another during this period of their marriage, which one is behaving as "adult"? "Child"? "Parent"? Did they switch back and forth between various roles? Are there any parallels between Abraham/Sarah and African American families today?

4. The Covenant and Birth of Isaac (Genesis 17:1-22; 21:1-14)

The Lord renewed His covenant with Abraham at the same time that He gave him a son.

a. What covenant did God make with Abraham? (17:1-14)

b. What promises did God make concerning the marriage of Abraham and Sarah? (17:15-22)

c. How did Abraham possibly contradict himself in his response to the Lord's promise? (17:17, 19-27) How did Sarah respond? (17:11-15)

d. How would you characterize Abraham's faith during this period? (20:1-18)

e. What problems followed the birth of Isaac? (21:1-14)

f. SUMMARY QUESTION: How would you classify the way in which Abraham and Sarah relate to one another during the above phase of their marriage? Did they switch back and forth between "child," "parent," and "adult"? Are there any parallels between Abraham/Sarah and African American families today?

5. Abraham's Test of Faith and the Death of Sarah (Genesis 17:15-17; 22:1-13; 23:1-4, 15-20)

After having progressed through many struggles, Abraham's faith is much stronger near the end of his life.

a. What did God ask Abraham to do? (22:1-2)

b. How did Abraham respond? (22:1-8)

c. In what ways did Abraham's response to the Lord demonstrate that he had matured in faith? (17:15-17; 22:1-8)

d. How might this encounter with the Lord have caused Abraham to have more mature faith? (22:1-13)

e. What other significant event took place during this stage of Abraham's life? (23:1-4, 15-20)

f. SUMMARY QUESTION: Why are Abraham and Sarah included in the Hebrews "Faith Hall of Fame"? (Hebrews 11:8-13) Can any parallels be drawn between Abraham, Sarah, and seniors within the African American church? What might seniors be able to teach younger people about the Lord, marriage, and faith in God?

6. FAMILY MINISTRY APPLICATION

Suppose your church were to develop a new marriage enrichment support group (if it doesn't already have one). Review this chapter and the story of Abraham and Sarah. Then list ten discussion topics that would be of interest to today's African American couples, and could be discussed in such a support group. Submit these to your director of Christian Education or pastor as possibilities for a new ministry at your church.

7. PERSONAL APPLICATION

What lessons can you draw from Abraham's and Sarah's faith journeys? What applications can you make to your personal life, whether married or single?

CHAPTER FIVE

PARENTING AFRICAN AMERICAN CHILDREN

"The child hates him who gives it all it wants."
(African Proverb)

It was Thursday night, and Jenny, 25, had just come in from choir rehearsal at her church. She and Alfred, her live-in boyfriend, sat silently in the living room, as her 13-year-old son Richard's stereo blasted from his room upstairs.

Jenny sat recalling how she had never married Richard's father, and she had been divorced from her husband, Richard's stepfather, for about a year now. She wondered if she should blame herself for what was happening. She was trying to be a good mother, but she couldn't find a job, and she felt that she had to depend on Alfred and the AFDC for help.

Almost a month ago Alfred had given Jenny the money to purchase Richard's "back to school" clothes. Jenny had noticed that, since Richard was a teenager, he wanted to spend more money for clothes. Jenny didn't know teens would spend quite as much as they did on clothes, but she was glad Alfred had given her the money. She had misgivings about it, but was outvoted. So Jenny and Alfred bought Richard a leather coat, some expensive tennis shoes, and several other items, in addition to paying for an expensive new haircut in the latest style.

Jenny had thought that, with as much money as she and her boyfriend spent on Richard, he couldn't help but make them proud. Therefore, it was a total shock to her when she learned that the reason Richard wanted the black leather jacket was because he belonged to a gang that wore black leather. In fact, Richard had joined the gang over the summer and had been hanging around with them while Jenny and Alfred were at work.

Alfred had told Jenny that just this morning, Richard's teacher had called and said Richard had been skipping his classes, he was already earning failing grades, and one of the other parents had complained that Richard had been seen at their home alone, with their daughter, while they were at work.

Suddenly Alfred jumped up from the couch and stormed upstairs to Richard's bedroom. Jenny ran after him, but was unable to stop him. Within minutes, Alfred and Richard were in a fist fight, and Alfred bruised Richard's face. Blood was all over the bed. Alfred was holding Richard down on the bed, threatening to kill him. Then, just as suddenly as it started, Alfred jumped up from the bed and stormed out the front door, heading for the bar down the street where he had been spending most of his evenings lately. Jenny didn't expect him to return too soon, if at all that night. That had been his pattern recently. She stood there crying, knowing that things were completely out of control.

Situations like this point to the need for parents to be taught how to parent. In some homes, both children and their parents are out of control. That is because most people assume the most responsible task of their lives, that of parenting, without any systematic training. Those who came from lovingly disciplined families which transmitted spiritual values and communicated well, had a good beginning. In addition, in most homes, family members have discounted the effects of societal factors on the functioning of the family unit. Therefore as conflict and problems arise they turn on each other, further diminishing their ability to cope. Rather we must help others cling together, identify the causes and consequences and solve problems together.

This chapter focuses on a few key areas of child rearing that are particularly challenging. It also reviews issues that are specific to African American families. It is designed for family members, church members and counselors who are concerned about equipping parents to parent.

Societal Factors Affecting Black Families. There have always been effective Black parents. In fact, McAdoo (1987) and other researchers have pointed to extended families and the Black church as the major sources of strength for Black families throughout the years. However, during the past twenty years a series of changes has occurred in the American economy and culture, the after effects of which have made it difficult for African American parents to function well as parents. While these factors have had an impact on all families, low-income parents have suffered more. These factors can be classified in terms of those which originate from without, and those which impact the family and originate from within. Obviously many of these are interdependent and affect each other. From without, families are affected by:

a) The American economy (declining purchasing power of the dollar, high costs of home ownership, unemployment rates).

b) Migration patterns of businesses and people breaking down the extended family and a sense of neighborhood.

c) Both parents working without adequate child care.

d) The popular media—its images and messages.

e) Deterioration of the Black community.

f) Deterioration of the schools.

g) Non-scriptural, Eurocentric concept of Christianity.

From within, families are affected by:

a) Premature sexual activity and pregnancy among youth.

b) Increasing divorce rates.

c) Prevalence of alcohol and drug abuse.

d) Lack of involvement with church and spiritual values.

e) Lack of a sense of belonging and interdependence with the Black community.

As a result of conditions from without, some African American families are finding themselves without enough food and clothing, with inadequate shelter, and with frequent shutoffs of basic utilities such as telephones, gas and electricity. They also find it difficult to obtain adequate education or job training in career fields that will enable long-term independent living. As a result, many nuclear families are being forced to migrate away from their extended families in order to seek employment and find resources. This is resulting in the gradual breakdown of strong African American extended families. Moreover, mothers are being forced to work outside of the family, making them unavailable to parent children at critical developmental stages. Salaries are often insufficient to provide adequate child and after school care.

A December 1990 research study from the Joint Center for Political and Economic Studies reports that nearly half of the nation's Black children live below the poverty line and are sinking deeper into poverty. Contrary to popular opinion the increase in female-headed households does not fully account for the increase. Of great concern was a conclusion of the study by Dr. Cynthia Rexroat, that children do not grow out of poverty, but usually spend their childhood and youth living under the accumulative burdens of poverty.

Also impacting from without is the general deterioration of inner city communities, where tax dollars are not being spent to rebuild and develop these areas. In these communities, both white collar crime and street crime exist alongside illegal drug traffic. Jobs no longer exist. Within these same communities, schools are not functioning as they should. There is a resulting breakdown in communication and influence between parents and the schools. Then there is the growing underclass of men and women who cannot find permanent employment, because they lack the skills to compete in the highly technological environment of today's workplace.

To add to all of this, families are bombarded by low moral standards which are transmitted on an hourly basis over television, in movies, and through music. They have seen and read of leaders in religion, government and the professions who have engaged in immoral behavior.

Then there are the pressures which impact the Black family from within. Greater sexual activity among youth results in premature pregnancies and an increase in teenaged mothers and fathers who are unprepared for parenthood. Increasing divorce rates lead to the presence of more single parents and the absence of fathers from the homes. Moreover, there is a decline in the involvement of many families with the Black church, and/or a limit to the amount of influence the church is allowed to have in the lives of its members. An overemphasis upon individualism to the neglect of community responsibility has pervaded the mentality of many. It has promoted a distorted sense of religion, a dangerous sense of classism and the myth that through separation from their heritage they can find freedom. Middle class people are supported and sometimes alienated from low-income families.

With societal factors having negative impacts from without and within the Black family, the responsibilities of parenting have become increasingly complex within our technical information age. Self-centeredness, demands for immediate gratification, and non-spiritual values continue to have a major impact on the Black family, as they do on all families. Parents must work longer and harder for economic survival as well as supplement the education of their children.

They are called upon to do all of this, in addition to participating in church activities, contributing to the community, and being the loving parents in their children's lives. As increasing demands and fewer services are available to parents, many are overwhelmed or burnt out from these high expectations. Black families in all economic classes raise their children within a racist society where every institution has been influenced by white superiority.

The Relationship Between Black Church and Black Family. Black families have traditionally not only defined family differently but have also appreciated it most greatly. Therein was one of two places where they could escape oppression and genuinely be treated as people of worth. These attitudes must be reclaimed through assisting parents and children in learning how to transmit spiritual values and treat one another so that bonding, purpose, inspiration and hope can unify them. If the African-American family does not survive as such, a people perish.

Children must be taught to seek after God. The quest for truth, the thirst to be reunited with God and become an instrument for His purposes on this earth should be believed and taught by some persons within the family. Parents must be reminded that their children should be brought to Sunday School, Vacation Bible School, and other youth groups. In years past, when Black families were strong, their lives revolved around the activities of the church, where they were in charge of determining their priorities and plotting their course.

Recitations and Sunday School reinforced reading and speaking. Christmas and Easter were more religious than secular. Children were in a protected environment safe from the influence of the street. This heritage must be reclaimed by Christian families and

96

through their outreach to neighbors. Indeed these efforts will prove futile unless churches are prepared to serve contemporary parents and children with relevancy and meaning as the Black church of old did. Leadership which is in touch with the daily lives of the community and responsive to it must continue emerging.

The Content of a Church-Based Parenting Ministry. Such a ministry would be shaped to address specific needs of African American parents. First order needs, such as food, shelter, clothing and health have escalated in cost so that parents now need help in budget management and consumer savvy in order to survive. People living in low-income neighborhoods generally do not have easy access to lower priced supermarkets, for instance. Limited dollars often prevent buying in large quantities at discount stores.

Therefore the church might want to develop a ministry that offers a weekly shopping day for church buses to take people shopping. The church could also organize purchasing cooperatives where food could be purchased in large quantities and made available for purchase to low-income families. The group purchasing trips would require that African Americans learn to plan and work together. The church might discover that there is a need for related literacy training as well, so parents can learn to read and compute as it relates to their survival in the marketplace. Developing networks with Black businesses and coalitions of similarly motivated people must be a future strategy.

General adult survival courses can be a part of a church-based ministry to families. In these courses, the importance of a wholesome breakfast before school, and the relationship between nutrition and health would be stressed for all family members, given the high incidence of hypertension, cancer, and heart disease in our community. Consumer savvy in how and where to obtain credit, purchase automobiles, and obtain automobile repairs are all important topics. They are particularly important, seeing that African Americans are often victims of unscrupulous people. A recent poll revealed that whether buying from a Black or white car salesperson, Blacks pay more in purchasing cars.

Another aspect of ministry to families involves activism. Churches can actively monitor businesses which do not offer quality products and services to their members and publicize the results of their surveys. If purchases are made in a large block, they can combine their monitoring with economic pressure in order to bring about change where needed. Advocacy for city, state, and federal services, accountability of all of our representatives and leaders are all legitimate functions of family outreach.

Collaboration and education are building blocks in assisting families in helping themselves provide for their children's basic needs. There are also church funds which can be redirected from less relevant purposes to providing assistance to children and youth. These include group health insurance, health fairs which offer free blood pressure screening, cholesterol testing, and immunizations, and libraries and computers for student use. Meetings can include meals, bread baskets can be provided, and used clothing sales can be sponsored by the family ministry of the church.

Part of family ministry is also providing for the educational and spiritual needs of children. Churches can survey the needs of the church and neighborhood to determine the need for African based Boy/Girl Scouts, sports leagues, etc. Churches can be open for young people after school for homework supervision, recreation, group dialogue time and snacks. Children and youth need activities. If we don't want them in the streets, then the church must provide a place for them.

Topics for Parenting Seminars and Courses. A parenting ministry can create a list of topics such as:

a) Education of Children

"How to Raise High Achieving Children"

"Developing Academic Self-Confidence"

"Teaching Children to Think Critically"
"Science and Mathematics Experiments at Home"
b) Special Celebrations and Rituals
"Passages into Manhood/Womanhood"
"Holiday Rituals for Spiritual Families"
c) Sex Education and Family Life
"Biblical Sexuality"
"Venereal Diseases Including AIDS"
"Old Testament Studies of Family Life: A Comparison"
"How to Teach Children About Their Bodies"
d) Substance Abuse
"How to Have Fun Without Drinking"
e) General
"Goal Setting for Family Members"
"Effective Communication within the Family"
"Parenting Children with Special Needs"
"Parenting Children with Disabilities"

More Specific Resources for Parenting Ministries. Through multiple approaches, by means of class instruction, workshops, films, dramas, retreats, camps, music, demonstrations and support groups we should develop a Christian Education program aimed at preparing young males and females for parenthood, child care classes for expecting parents, parenting skills programs for those actively parenting, and grandparent/relatives programs for those secondarily aiding others in parenting their young. Specialized support/recovery groups should be cropping up all over the church and community where sharing and inner healing can take place.

Shadowing techniques, in which inexperienced parents are brought together with experienced parents in order to observe how to prepare for a teacher conference, supervise school work, teach a child to read, conduct family devotions, discipline a child, build self-confidence, etc., are particularly helpful because adults are shown, not just told. They can then adapt and individualize a procedure or process to the particulars of their personal situation.

Infusing African American History into a Parenting Ministry. African American psychologist Wade Nobles discusses the unique requirement of Black parents to raise healthy children under a racist system. He writes, "...the family parent-child relationship will have to center on the creation and maintenance of three senses: the sense of history, the sense of family, and the sense of the ultimate supreme power (God)" (Nobles, 1981, *Black Families,* p. 83). Nobles points out the necessity for African American children to be taught their African history which has been left out of the education of most people.

They need to know that their history did not begin with the humiliation of slavery but that as Africans they are the descendants of the first civilization in the world who contributed to the origins of science, mathematics, philosophy, language, government and spirituality. This enables them to know their true identity, not that which was created for them in the Americas. Such knowledge would empower them to answer the crucial questions of: Who am I? Why am I here? What is my role? Where is my place?

These questions begin to be raised with the onset of puberty. It is at that point in early adolescence when some of our youth feel most alienated and directionless.

A sense of history and their place in it must be supplied by the home as educated by the church. The dissemination of African and African American history can be directed to the complete extended family during church family nights. Parents who may not attend a preaching service may eagerly respond to an informal seminar on this topic.

Nurturing Children. Instinctively our former generations of grandmothers and mothers knew how to mother babies. They responded with good common sense. However we now have in-

100

creasingly younger fathers and mothers who do not have good common parenting sense. They still need nurturing themselves. Parents need training in how to effectively parent beginning even before the baby is born. Early childhood education is necessary in order to provide a sense of order and trust within the child. As the infant develops they need stimulation of the senses. As they grow they continue to require love and guidance. Parents must learn to create bonds with their children by talking to them, planting dreams, purpose and hope. These are some of the skills about which our teenage parents usually have not the remotest idea and must be taught. Parents who have been victims of abuse often need special help and support in order not to repeat what was done to them when under stress.

Fathers as well as mothers, whether married or not must be included in parenting education. African American young men must be taught and held accountable for bringing children into the world as they are taught the meaning and measure of a true man.

Helping Children Cope with Divorce. At certain critical periods in the life of a child, if the parents divorce it seems to have a more troubling affect than at other times. We know that divorce effects young children more severely. During the first year after divorce, there is an increase in anxiety in young children. With boys we see more acting out and rebelliousness during the first year. We often find girls withdrawing during the first year. At all ages, however, children seem to carry an unconscious sense that they were responsible for the divorce. They think that somehow they contributed to it. Some are haunted by memories of when they misbehaved and link these times with reasons for the family failure.

In fact, if you talk with children right after a divorce, we discover that they hold the fantasy that somehow the divorced parents will reunite. The possible exception is the child in an abusive situation. They dream about this, repeat it to you, and often try to manipulate their parents into reuniting.

This is one reason the parent/counselor must be aware of the effects of divorce on children. They need to be alerted to children's illnesses, mood shifts, lower school grades, gang membership, changes in behavior, withdrawal, suicidal tendencies, and so forth. We are still researching the effects on children of never having lived with their father. Much of the effect on children will probably have to do with the life-style of the family and whether there are other members who can come in and offer direction and support. The strong, active role of a grandfather, uncle or older brother has made a difference in the lives of African Americans in the past.

Providing ongoing opportunities for children to discuss their feelings is helpful. Encouraging contact with the missing parent is good if abuse did not take place. Not forcing the child to take sides is healthy. Conducting sessions which permit sharing the feelings of loss are useful for those youth separated from a missing parent for whatever reason.

Overseeing the Education of Children. Parents need to know what has an effect on the ability of their child to learn. Children of low-income parents are sometimes placed in special education programs where they get detoured from the mainstream. They are limited from the time they enter school as to what their choices will be later. These children are not being given the same curriculum in those classes as other children get. Parents must be involved in their children's education and provide a home environment for learning. Parents must supplement public education. This requires assistance from the church.

Parents need to know how to get their children back into the mainstream of education if they are to succeed. Their children may have the ability, but they may not be given the chance or may not be studying effectively. Many of these children are labeled as learning disabled, EMH, attention deficit disordered, and hyperactive. Some of these are the children that our grandparents thought were very bright, but for whom we had to keep things changing, and whom we had to stimulate because they were highly imaginative and precocious. Others need individual tutoring and learning specialists who can discover the child's method of processing information and devise an appropriate instructional strategy. Every child needs a quiet place to study and periodic resources such as books, materials and human assistance. An after school church program is vital.

Nutrition is very important, particularly for the hyperactive child who has been labeled as having an attention deficit disorder. The nature of the home, the stability of the home, and whether the home is regulated and secure are all factors that affect these children. Such children need an order with which they can identify. It is more likely in the home of the single family that this may not be taking place simply because there are fewer adults to oversee homework and supervise the life of the child. Some parents have returned to school themselves in order to better assist their children.

Parenting the Developing Child. For the child in the middle years (ages 6-12) growth in his identifications with his peers (age mates) and with the family should be taking place. The peer group provides the security and the models which smooth the passage from dependence on parents to increasing separation from his/her parents and launches then into the adolescent world. Dangers of peer influence occur when the child does not learn how to say no to activities which are contrary to his Christian beliefs. Too much dependence upon the group may cause the child never to stand on his own two feet, make decisions, or walk alone when necessary. The desire to belong can lead to dangerous experimentation. Excessive demands upon parents may cause the child to wear designer, grown-up clothing styles or enter early into adolescent activities.

It is normal for children in this age range to experience sibling rivalry, resulting in arguments and jealousy among themselves, much to the consternation of parents. Parents of teenagers need to be able to band together in a support group. Solidarity with peers often leads to secrecy and the questioning of parental

103

beliefs and traditions. They may perceive these as old fashioned and outdated. Parents must sort through these and be firm in those values which are unchanging and absolute. Parents must know their children's friends, activities and whereabouts. That is responsible parenting which becomes much easier if the family operates within a "community" or "network" of church families.

There are two major areas in which problems generally first express themselves for the preadolescent child—school and the street. The struggle is psychological, mental, and spiritual. It has to do with experiencing academic competence versus experiencing feelings of inferiority due to lack of accomplishment. It also has to do with whether the child feels he has an impact and place in his/her environment. A signal of problems is a child having a prolonged academic or adjustment problem. The contributing factors should be investigated and intervention brought to bear before it also becomes an emotional problem. Parents need to be aware of their preadolescent child's school life and ethical development. What attitudes and view of the world are they developing? How are they integrating all the things they hear, read, and see?

Success at school demands meeting academic expectations as well as learning to get along with other children, teachers, and with a system which may be different from their home environment. If a child frequently resists going to school or has numerous illnesses, the parent should discover the causes. Preadolescent children who feel inferior or unloved or lack basic academic skills are vulnerable for more serious problems. Those who never accept responsibility for their actions, saying that their actions are always someone else's fault, become immature or self-righteous. They also are in need of corrective thinking.

In today's world preadolescent children also encounter problems in the street. These problems were previously encountered by older teenagers. These include induction into gang life, becoming runners for drug pushers, being approached as sexual objects, participating in robberies, and using drugs.

Runaway children often turn inward, withdraw from the real world and/or act out rebelliously out of hurt and anger. They and their parents require counseling in working through their feelings and behaviors. This type of support may be needed to cope with any major change in the child's life. Any respected person or member of the church may be the one to whom the family turns. Hence the need for a church to have an internal referral system to help very troubled family members. This internal system would be aware of and work cooperatively with responsible referral resources in the community.

The child who commits aggressive and/or violent acts without a sense of remorse may already have very serious problems. These children, who steal or lie habitually, often without a parental benefit to themselves, probably have long-term problems. A conscience seems to be lacking because they may deny an act you saw them commit! These behaviors demand professional help immediately.

The absence of apparent problems does not necessarily indicate the presence of good emotional health. The elementary age child should be growing in skill competencies, self-confidence, internal control, discipline, concern for others, independence, appropriate sex role development, and selection of friends. Equally as important, the child should be moving toward a personalized belief system which offers a philosophy of life relevant to his and others' needs and which is adequate for the challenges of life today.

Modeling Christ for Children. Parents must learn to introduce to children and model for them the life of Christ in human vessels. Only Christ Himself can provide them with a source of life within, and with individualized direction for the future. This ideally occurs before the onslaught of the turmoil of the adolescent years.

Raising Children in the Urban Environment. Raising children in an urban environment has been the subject of many articles. Many of these articles have focused on raising African

American children. The simple fact is that 20th century urban living is confusing to say the least, and raising children in it is even more complicated. This is because parents are uncertain of the future. They are subjected to many rapid changes to which they cannot adjust and over which they have little control. They are frightened because our world has created social monsters which prey upon them and their families. Children must be taught survival skills, especially Black male children, given the increased attacks on their survival. They need to clearly understand how the system works in general and who it works specifically in relationship to them as Blacks. Whether they are aspiring to be a congressman, minister or truck driver Black teenage males between 15 and 25 years old need the guidance of stable Black males in their homes.

Communities, School and Churches. This special population must have priority as we define our mission. Strength and promise are to be found in Proverbs 22:6, which charges us to "train up a child in the way he should go, and when he is old he will not depart from it." How important it is to be led by Him who holds the future in His hand.

Preparing Children for the 21st Century. How can we prepare children for the 21st century? Let's examine just a few of the things with which our children must cope in the 21st century. As new information is disseminated about our history and as Western society continues to disintegrate our children must be resocialized or reeducated, using Western and non-Western content that offers new ways of living and solving problems. Then there is technology which is altering the workplace and bringing with it the need for lifelong learning. At the present rate of technological advancement, changes will occur even more rapidly than before. Since humanity has historically resisted the inner changes necessary to adjust to external changes, the gap between changes and personal adjustment will continue to widen. Americans must clearly learn to modify their way of life—its excesses for many, and its disregard for the poor and the environment.

The Bible clearly teaches us that the future will grow worse. All these issues indicate that the stresses we now have will intensify rather than improve. How then do we train children to cope with these expected conditions? Some say that all a child needs is God and all other things will be provided. We suggest that it is not enough to ask a child merely to accept Christ. We must go beyond that and teach what it means to accept Christ, what it means to really "know" God, and how God fits into their daily lives as it relates to their goals, the nature of their relationships and the causes they champion.

We cannot teach a child this if we do not know the difference between a true believer and one who pretends to know God. We have to know that when you know God, the person of Christ comes into your life. It is like being pregnant in the sense that you cannot be half-pregnant, you either are or are not pregnant. Jesus Himself put it best when He dictates that you must be either cold or hot. The lukewarm will discard. The body of a pregnant woman changes from the moment she becomes pregnant. She is not the same again for the duration of the pregnancy and probably not the same ever again. The woman gives her body totally to harbor a new life, and commits every aspect of her body to all the changes necessary to nourish that life.

In like manner, when a person becomes a Christian he makes a commitment to have a new life within himself. When that happens, changes will occur that are necessary to sustain that new life. It is in recognition of this that our ancestors adhered to the principles of "Maat" which thousands of years later Jesus used in His reply to the question, "Which is the greatest commandment?" He said the greatest commandment was to love God with everything we have and to love our neighbor as ourselves. Our ancestors made sure that by the time a child became an adult he/she had incorporated the principles of Maat in his or her life. The ruler himself or herself became the daily living model through his or her rulership.

This then is what we need to do with our children. Our church (spiritual) leaders must become our daily living models, parents must follow such models in parenting, and we must have rituals and celebrations to go with it. Now, being a model does not require any supernatural behavior, or a life free of mistakes. But it does mean having life that manifests the principle of Maat which Jesus manifested in its perfect form. It means when we make a mistake we accept it and correct it. It means that if we dislike or hate a person just because of his nationality or race, we recognize it and actively do whatever is necessary to overcome such hatred. It means we recognize that we are human, but because the Spirit lives in us we are capable of correcting our human failures in a way that maintains harmony within the Christian community and the human community at large.

In our Sunday schools, vacation Bible schools, even in the worship services we must teach biblical principles so that our children do more than quote chapter and verse. We can settle for nothing less than seeing our Black children understanding and incorporating these principles in their lives.

We must also teach them flexibility. Throughout history, those who survived change were those who were flexible. Being flexible does not mean compromising one's principles; it only means having a variety of resources, so that one can use a variety of strategies to solve problems. One also needs the ability to look at the other side of issues. This will enable them to adjust to changes and new environments, and problem solve creatively. We need to raise children who can fit into an international world, strongly rooted in their own heritage and able to think critically and globally.

We also must help children develop a good self-image and pride in their cultural heritage. This leads to self-confidence which enables them to set goals and persist against obstacles to their completion. It does not connote selfishness or superiority. It does mean that in a world where black continues to mean inferiority and white superiority, we must consciously teach our children to value themselves, have faith in themselves and maintain a sense of hope.

It says to our children and parents that I am somebody, I am important, and I am special. God came to earth and died to tell us that we are all individually important, special, somebodies. If, then, God created me an African, and died to tell me that as an African I am important and special, why in the world can I not be proud of who I am? To do less than that is to remain in psychological and mental slavery. Should not all people feel this way?

So it is our responsibility to teach our children to be proud of who they are. This is all the more important, seeing that they are bombarded with media images which portray them often as pimps, criminals, drug abusers, and low achievers individually and as a people. It is particularly important as African American people to understand who we are, what our purpose in the world is, and why we have gone through the experiences we have had. This self-knowledge will help us prepare for our future and when we understand the future, we will be able to cope with it much better and prepare our children for it.

Summary. This chapter has focused on parenting skills. It has presented several attitudes needed by African American parents of today, and has presented guidelines for meeting the challenges related to raising children with these skills. Following is an exercise which allows you to apply principles covered in this chapter to the study of several generations of biblical parents.

BIBLE FAMILIES

INSTRUCTIONS: Following are exercises which allow you to apply the principles covered in this chapter to several generations of biblical parents. The first five exercises consist of five "fill-in-the-blank" discovery questions and a summary question. The sixth exercise helps you to apply the knowledge gained, to develop a church-based family ministry. The seventh exercise provides opportunity for personal application.

Eli, Hophni and Phinehas

"Now the sons of Eli were sons of Belial; they knew not the Lord. Wherefore the sin of the young men was very great before the Lord: for men abhorred the of- fering of the Lord. Now Eli was very old, and heard all that his sons did unto all Israel; and how they lay with the women that assembled at the door of the taber- nacle of the congregation. And the ark of God was taken; and the two sons of Eli, Hophni and Phinehas, were slain. And it came to pass, when he [a mes- senger] made mention of the ark of God, that he [Eli] fell from off the seat backward by the side of the gate, and his neck brake, and he died." (1 Samuel 2:12, 17, 22; 4:11, 18)

Elkanah, Hannah and Samuel

"Now there was a certain man...and his name was Elkanah...And he had two wives; the name of the one was Hannah, and the name of the other Penin- nah...Wherefore it came to pass...after Hannah had con- ceived, that she bare a son, and called his name Samuel...And when she had weaned him, she...brought him unto the house of the Lord in Shiloh:

"And she said, Oh my lord, as thy soul liveth, my lord, I am the woman that stood by thee here, praying unto the Lord. For this child I prayed; and the Lord hath given me my petition which I asked of him: Therefore also I have lent him to the Lord; as long as he liveth he shall be lent to the Lord. And he wor-

110

shipped the Lord there. And Elkanah went to Ramah to his house. And the child did minister unto the Lord before Eli the priest. And the child Samuel grew on, and was in favour both with the Lord, and also with men." (1 Samuel 1:1-2, 20, 24, 26-28; 2:11, 26)

Samuel, Joel, and Abiah

"And it came to pass, when Samuel was old, that he made his sons judges over Israel. Now the name of his firstborn was Joel; and the name of the second, Abiah: they were judges in Beersheba. And his sons walked not in his ways, but turned aside after lucre, and took bribes, and perverted judgment. Then all the elders of Israel gathered themselves together, and came to Samuel unto Ramah, And said unto him, Behold, thou art old, and thy sons walk not in thy ways: now make us a king to judge us like all the nations.

"Now the Lord...told Samuel...Tomorrow about this time I shall send thee a man out of the land of Benjamin, and thou shalt anoint him to be captain over my people Israel...And when Samuel saw Saul, the Lord said unto him, Behold the man whom I spake to thee of! this same shall reign over my people." (1 Samuel 8:1-5; 9:15-17)

Saul and Jonathan

"And Saul spake to Jonathan his son, and to all his servants, that they should kill David. But Jonathan Saul's son delighted much in David: and Jonathan told

David, saying, Saul my father seeketh to kill thee: now therefore, I pray thee, take heed to thyself until the morning, and abide in a secret place, and hide thyself:

"And Jonathan spake good of David unto Saul his father, and said unto him, Let not the king sin against his servant, against David; because he hath not sinned against thee, and because his works have been to theeward very good: And Saul hearkened unto the voice of Jonathan: and Saul sware, As the Lord liveth, he shall not be slain. Then Saul's anger was kindled against Jonathan, and he said unto him...For as long as the son of Jesse liveth...thou shalt not be established, nor thy kingdom...And Jonathan answered Saul his father...Wherefore shall he be slain? what hath he done? And Saul cast a javelin at him to smite him:" (1 Samuel 19:1-2, 4, 6; 20:30-33)

David, Amnon, Absalom and Tamar

"And unto David were sons born in Hebron: and his firstborn was Amnon, of Ahinoam the Jezreelitess;...and the third, Absalom the son of Maacah the daughter of Talmai king of Geshur; And it came to pass after this, that Absalom the son of David had a fair sister, whose name was Tamar; and Amnon the son of David loved her. So Amnon lay down, and made himself sick...

"...And Tamar took the cakes which she had made, and brought them into the chamber to Amnon her brother. And when she had brought them unto him to eat, he took hold of her, and said unto her, Come lie

112

with me, my sister. And she answered him, Nay, my brother, do not force me; for no such thing ought to be done in Israel: do not thou this folly. Howbeit he would not hearken unto her voice: but, being stronger than she, forced her, and lay with her. And Absalom her brother said unto her, Hath Amnon thy brother been with thee?...

"And it came to pass after two full years... Absalom...commanded his servants, saying, Mark ye now when Amnon's heart is merry with wine, and when I say unto you, Smite Amnon; then kill him...And the servants of Absalom did unto Amnon as Absalom had commanded...But Absalom fled...And the soul of king David longed to go forth unto Absalom: for he was comforted concerning Amnon, seeing he was dead." (2 Samuel 3:2-3; 13:1, 6, 10-12, 14, 20, 23, 28-29, 37, 39)

1. Eli, Hophni and Phinehas (1 Samuel 2:12, 17, 22; 4:1, 18)

Eli's religious life did not seem to have an influence on his sons' spiritual lives.
a. From whom was Eli descended? (Leviticus 10:1, 2, 12; 1 Kings 2:27; 1 Chronicles 24:3; 2 Samuel 8:17)
b. Who were the sons of Eli, and what does the expression "sons of Belial" say about their character? (1 Samuel 1:1-3; 2:12, 17; Deuteronomy 13:3; Judges 12:22)
c. What was the environment surrounding Eli and his sons? (1 Samuel 1:9; 2:27-30; 7:6, 15-17)
d. Describe the problem that existed between Eli and his sons and describe the problems that it eventually caused the family and community. (1 Samuel 2:22-25, 27-36; 4:1, 18)
e. What seems to have been missing in Eli's parenting? (Proverbs 22:6; Ephesians 6:4)

113

f. SUMMARY QUESTION: Was Eli successful in relating his religious life to his private parenting life? Explain. In what ways are many modern Christian parents similar to Eli in their parenting styles?

2. Elkanah, Hannah and Samuel (1 Samuel 1:24, 27-28)

The temple became very involved with the parenting of Samuel, their son.

a. Describe Eli the priest's involvement with the parents of Samuel. (1 Samuel 1:9-18, 20-28; 2:11, 20-21)

b. What role did the Lord play in Hannah's life, and how might this have affected her mothering? (2:1-10, 19)

c. How was Eli the priest involved with the parenting of Samuel, and in what ways did he become a part of the extended family? (2:11, 18, 26; 3:1-20)

d. What role did Samuel eventually play in Israel? (7:1-17)

e. What was the rich family heritage of Samuel, and how might Eli have infused his cultural history into his religious education? What impact might this have had on Samuel? (1:1-2; 1 Chronicles 16:1, 26, 35; Genesis 29:34; Exodus 6:25; Numbers 8:6; Ezra 2:70; John 1:19)

f. SUMMARY QUESTION: What can African American parents learn from Eli, about infusing the history of God's interaction with African Americans into the Christian education of their children?

3. Samuel, Joel and Abiah (1 Samuel 8:1-17)

It appears that Samuel had trouble relating his religious life to his private "parenting" life.

a. What problems may have existed between Samuel and his sons? (8:1-5)

b. What environment surrounded Samuel and his sons, and what effect might it have had on them? (7:1-17)

114

c. In what ways might Samuel's and Eli's (Samuel's mentor) jobs have interfered with the parenting of their sons? (2:26; 1:9; 4:16, 18; 7:15-17)

d. What happened as a result of Samuel's sons' behavior? (8:5-10; 9:15-17)

e. How were the outcomes of Samuel and Eli's problems similar? (2:12, 17; 4:14-18; 8:1-5; 10:27)

f. SUMMARY QUESTION: In the case of Eli and Samuel, how might parenting styles have been passed from generation to generation? To what extent does this happen in African American families today? What outcomes have been positive? What outcomes have been negative?

4. Saul, Ahinoam and Jonathan (1 Samuel 14:49-52; 9:1-6; 20:30-33)

Saul was a very insecure man. This insecurity had an effect on his career and on the parenting of his son, Jonathan.

a. What evidence is there that Saul was an insecure man? (9:25—10:1, 20-22; 18:5-11) How might this have affected his relationship with Jonathan?

b. Describe the type of environment surrounding Saul's family (14:49-52), and how this environment might have affected Jonathan. (13:2, 3; 14:1, 4-23)

c. What are some historical realities which might have caused Saul to be insecure? (1 Samuel 2:1-18; 22-26; 3:20; 4:17-18; 8:5-10; 9:15-17)

d. What types of messages about morality did Saul transmit to Jonathan? (14:24-45; 19:1-6; 20:25-33)

e. What was the ultimate outcome of Saul's insecurity in the position to which God had called him, and in his role as a parent? (29:1—31:1)

f. SUMMARY QUESTION: How was Saul's environment similar and different from environments surrounding Black families today? In what ways can this affect the way Black

115

people raise their children? What types of mistakes can be made? What does Christianity have to do with it?

5. David, Amnon, Absalom and Tamar (2 Samuel 3:3; 13:1, 6, 10-11, 14, 20, 23, 28-29, 37, 39)

David sent mixed signals to his children. On the one hand, he loved the Lord and served Him, on the other, he disobeyed the Lord in his relationships with women.

a. How many wives and related children did David have? (1 Samuel 27:3; 1 Chronicles 3:1; 2 Samuel 2-3; 1 Chronicles 3:1-4; 2 Samuel 5:15-16; 1 Chronicles 3:5-4; 14:4-5)

b. In the story of creation, what evidence is there that the Lord does not promote polygamy? (Genesis 2:21-25)

c. In addition to spending time with his many wives, what other involvements with women did David have? (2 Samuel 11:1—13:29)

d. In addition to spending time with women, what else did David do? (Psalm 3; 2 Samuel 2:1-11; 5:1-7)

e. Indirectly, what values did David transmit to Amnon and Absalom about sex, women and murder, and how did his mixed messages affect their later behavior? (13:1, 6, 10-11, 14, 20, 23, 28-29, 37, 39)

f. SUMMARY QUESTION: Today, the popular media promotes promiscuity, adultery and disrespect for human life. Draw parallels between the times in which David raised his children and today. What lessons can be learned from David's mistakes?

6. FAMILY MINISTRY APPLICATION

Review exercises #1-5. Visualize modern Black families that are similar to the biblical families studied. From these situations, develop a list of topics for some parenting seminars. The topics should allow parents to discuss the problems and brainstorm solutions.

7. PERSONAL APPLICATION

In what ways is your extended and/or nuclear family similar to the families studied in the above exercises? What principles can be learned from their situations and applied to yours?

CHAPTER SIX

TRANSMITTING VALUES

**"What the child says, he has heard it at home."
(African Proverb)**

As Mr. Jesse sat on his porch, watching the children across the street playing "double dutch," his mind wandered to the summer of 1954 when he was only 13 years old. He remembered watching his great-grandfather, Papa Jesse, in his eighties at the time, opening the evening newspaper and putting on his glasses. Mr. Jesse would never forget the look on Papa Jesse's face as he stared at the headlines.

"Whew! God answers prayer!" Papa Jesse had said, shaking his head. The headlines announced the Supreme Court's Brown vs. the Board of Education decision, making segregated schools illegal.

"They've finally turned the old Plessy vs. Ferguson decision around. You know that Plessy vs. Ferguson decision is what made it okay for white people to force Black children to go to segregated schools, where children couldn't get the same education as white children," he explained.

Mr. Jesse could still remember Papa Jesse's words. "Boy, I believe I was about your age when Plessy vs. Ferguson was passed. I never thought I'd see the day when the decision was turned around!"

A ring from the telephone in the next room brought

Mr. Jesse back to the present. He lifted the receiver, only to learn that Jesse, Jr., his 16-year-old son who had dropped out of high school recently, had been arrested with drugs again. He stood there, tears of anger filling his eyes, shaking his head.

One of the biggest contributors to the "generation gap" between parents, grandparents and youth is the seeming inability of some people to transmit values which they hold dear to their children. However, it is critical to the survival of African American youth that they reexamine the values of the older generation and make better choices as to the ones they will accept and reject.

Values are transmitted within the family. Therefore, this chapter focuses on the art of transmitting values within the family from parents to children. It will explore the concept of spiritual values in detail, and will present ways in which such values can be passed on by parents to their children. It is designed for parents and people who minister to parents, during the turbulent times in which we live.

What Values Are. Values are those concepts we consider worthwhile. They are the beliefs that society at large considers desirable and essential for functioning in society. Values are those beliefs which have been handed down through the ages and which society feels are desirable and essential for its survival.

Values include the ideas that form the fabric of individual behavior, and of the collective behavior of human culture. In a society, the collective behavior of the people is called culture. Culture reflects the values of a society. The same is true with communities such as the community of Christians.

The family is the social unit of our society where basic spiritual values should be taught. While Christian values are taught by the church, it is the church's primary responsibility to equip parents for their responsibilities. Spiritual values can best be taught by equipped parents because they can be interwoven with everyday life.

What Are Spiritual Values? The English word "spirit" comes from the Latin word *spiritus* which means "breath" or "wind." The Greeks used the word *pneuma* and the Hebrews used *ruahh*. All of these words were used to mean an "active force." Although the force itself may not be visible, the evidence of its presence is clearly visible. We do not see the wind, but we know it is present by what it does. Spirit, without any qualification, therefore, may be good or bad, but nevertheless is an active force. When Christians talk about "the Spirit," however, we mean the Spirit of God.

When we talk about spiritual values, we mean those desirable concepts or ideas which are a part of God's nature. These values are not passive but are instead very active. To acquire spiritual values means to acquire God's nature.

Again we must depart from commonly used language in order to appeal to the African American Christian to think and ask crucial questions which are necessary to grow spiritually. We do not believe that anybody who wants to know God or who has the Spirit of God in him needs to be afraid to ask God to answer his sincere questions. If we are going to transmit a value, it is imperative that we know and understand what that value is.

We live in a society where we use language as a substitute for understanding. If we use the right words to describe our faith, it is accepted that we have the correct relationship with God.

The Bible gives testimony to God. That testimony is that God created the universe and all that is in it. God created man in His own image. Sin separated man from God, who sent His Son, Jesus Christ, to reconcile man to Himself. Jesus, therefore, rekindled that image of God in man through His death and resurrection. Therefore, when you see redeemed persons you should in fact see the image of God in them.

A crucial question is if America is a Christian nation and Christianity pervades the society, why is there so little brotherhood? What are truly spiritual values and how can people claim a relationship with God and yet not reflect His nature? There has obviously been a misrepresentation of God in popular Christianity. It then becomes necessary for African Americans to prayerfully search for the true God. His nature and His teachings in the Scriptures constitute the values we must transmit to our children. To do anything less is to participate in the molestation of God that we see going on in many Christian churches around the world.

The Ways in Which Children Acquire Spiritual Values. Children take on spiritual values primarily through several means: instruction, identification with parents, imitation of others, practice of customs, family activities and through receiving rewards within the family. Through identification with parents, children take on aspects of parental behavior (their values). They learn other values from other adult role models in their lives. These adult role models are the people upon whom the child learns to depend. Because they want to be like these models, they absorb as a part of themselves what they think these role models are like. They tend to be influenced by those people in their environment who yield visible power and attractiveness. This is one reason why we must be selective about the people with whom our children spend time. We should be careful in this respect from the time the children are infants.

Children are great copiers. They mimic the people around them. If the family prays together or shows concern for others, children will begin imitating these behaviors. Children also develop a sense of what is important based upon what brings them rewards within the family. This is why it is important for parents to be aware of the kinds of behavior for which they give extra attention, praise, or cuddling.

Values also are transmitted through family customs and activities. What one chooses to do with one's day, week, and life is a reflection of what a person holds as important. If parents read the Bible at home, grapple with interpreting and applying it in their relationships and their world view, children come to sense that the Scriptures have usefulness for everyday life.

Simply telling someone to be truthful is hardly sufficient unless dishonesty has negative consequences and speaking the truth is rewarding. However the admonition not to lie can appear hypocritical if youth observe older family members being dishonest.

Values About Education. Historically African Americans have valued education. Immediately after the Emancipation Proclamation was read, freed slaves sought education. Some of their first purchases were for a slate and pencil so that they could be taught to read. Great-grandparents and grandparents suffered in order to send their children to school. Between 1967 and 1976 there was a 246% increase in the enrollment of Black students in college. A decline followed, leading to only a 6.1% increase between 1976 and 1982. It gradually reached a standstill and then declined.

Noticeably absent are Black males. We now know that more are under the jurisdiction of the courts than are in college. Our male youth are dropping out either physically or mentally during the latter half of elementary school in far too many cases. It is critical that we assist families in once again making quality education a highly desirable value in the lives of our children.

"Real Life" Issues. People face a real dilemma when they realize that they cannot be honest with "significant others" without the threat of loss of love. What greater conflict this poses for children and youth. However, a home atmosphere which encourages open discussion with family members (or a Sunday School class) around issues of peer pressure, temptations, value conflicts and problem solving is an essential training ground for young people.

Church people are often frightened when youths present real life issues and situations. All too often they respond by wanting to silence them, or "straighten them out" right away. This behavior on the part of adults is seen by youth as condemnation and judgment. Young people faced with this situation quickly learn that, when talking to adults, they can only discuss certain topics, namely they cannot discuss the real things troubling them. It is important that these issues are examined and explored. Through the use of drama, role playing, and debates, young people can be permitted to examine values and practice making decisions based on biblical truth.

A person's behavior, budget allocations and time priorities are more accurate indicators to young people of an adult's values than the adult's public testimony on Wednesday night. When young people observe a contradiction between values and behavior, this causes them to lose faith in adults and ultimately it affects their ability to trust God.

The following poem is based on 1 Corinthians 13:4-8, and it illustrates how Scripture helps us relate to others, relate to our positions within society and develop policies for helping others:

I will be patient with you
I will be kind to you
I will not envy you
I will not boast or proudly elevate myself above you
I will not be rude to you
I will not exploit you for my own selfish ends
I will not be easily angered with you
I will keep no record of wrongs
I will not delight when you are harmed or I hear evil concerning you
I will rejoice with truth
I will always protect you
I will always trust you
I will always hope in you
I will persevere with you
I will never fail you.
(author unknown)

Values About Marriage. Given the unique nature of our experience in America and recent secular influences, particular values related to male/female relationships need to be internalized by young people while they are within their nuclear families. One such value is marital fidelity and commitment. This value is based on the recognition that the purpose of marriage and family is not merely for personal pleasure and romantic love. Personal pleasure and romantic love are distinctly self-centered and usually short-lived.

God ordained family life for a greater purpose: the glory and honor of Himself. Through the family we have a network of relationships which become a vehicle for developing transformed thinking and behavior. The family prepares us to move out into the world as intentional witnesses.

Both the Scriptures and our African heritage teach us to respect women, raise wise men, revere and care for the aged, strive for excellence and work hard. Many families are no longer teaching or practicing these values. Caring people must help restore these values in African American families where they no longer exist.

The Role of the Family in Teaching Spiritual Values. It follows that when a family clearly demonstrates spiritual values in its daily life, it becomes easier for children to understand what God is truly like. Like the parents, they then will want to be like Jesus also. Parents can become the guides for leading their children into a personal relationship with God through Jesus Christ if they know Him. The church can serve as the backup and support system for assisting parents in training their children.

The home and church are designed to work as a team, with the home enriching the church and the church equipping the home. For non-Christian families, the outreach ministry must do that which a family is unable to do. God has assigned to the family the task of helping children take on the characteristics of God's nature. He regards godly living as an important and desirable part of a person's life. One's home then becomes God's workshop for preparing the family to make a decision to accept and follow Jesus Christ. It is here we begin the growth process of being disciplined.

The Christian family has the primary responsibility of providing opportunities and encouraging the development of the following spiritual values: a) faith and confidence in God; b) loving submission to Him; c) social responsibility to others; d) a life purpose centered around God's plan for the individual and the world; e) a desire to seek the truth; f) fairness in all dealings; and g) commitment to high moral principles.

Summary. This chapter has focused on the transmission of values. It has discussed how spiritual values are transmitted to children, and how the family can teach spiritual values. Following is an exercise which allows the reader to apply the principles presented in this chapter to the study of a biblical family.

BIBLE FAMILIES

INSTRUCTIONS: The following exercises allow you to apply principles from this chapter to the study of a biblical family. The first five exercises consist of five "fill-in-the-blank" discovery questions and a summary question. The sixth exercise helps you apply the knowledge gained to a church-based family ministry. The seventh exercise allows for personal application.

The Sons of Jacob and Rachel

"Now Israel loved Joseph more than all his children, because he was the son of his old age: and he made him a coat of many colours. And when his brethren saw that their father loved him more than all his brethren, they hated him, and could not speak peaceably unto him. And Joseph dreamed a dream, and he told it his brethren: and they hated him yet the more." (Genesis 37:3-5)

126

"And [they] sold Joseph to the Ishmeelites for twenty pieces of silver: and they brought Joseph into Egypt." (37:28)

"And the Lord was with Joseph, and he was a prosperous man; and he was in the house of his master the Egyptian. And Joseph found grace in his sight, and he served him: and he made him overseer over his house, and all that he had he put into his hand." (39:2, 4)

The Children of Jochebed and Levi

"And the name of Amram's wife was Jochebed, the daughter of Levi, whom her mother bare to Levi in Egypt: and she bare unto Amram Aaron and Moses, and Miriam their sister." (Numbers 26:59)

"...And Aaron cast down his rod before Pharaoh, and before his servants, and it became a serpent. Then Pharaoh also called the wise men and the sorcerers: now the magicians of Egypt, they also did in like manner with their enchantments. For they cast down every man his rod, and they became serpents: but Aaron's rod swallowed up their rods." (Exodus 7:10-12)

"And Moses stretched out his hand over the sea; and the Lord caused the sea to go back by a strong east wind all that night, and made the sea dry land, and the waters were divided. And the children of Israel went into the midst of the sea upon the dry ground: and the waters were a wall unto them on their right hand, and on their left." (Exodus 14:21-22)

"And Miriam the prophetess, the sister of Aaron, took a timbrel in her hand; and all the women went

out after her with timbrels and with dances. And Miriam answered them, Sing ye to the Lord, for he hath triumphed gloriously; the horse and his rider hath he thrown into the sea." (15:20-21)

The Children of Ahab and Jezebel

"Ahaziah the son of Ahab began to reign over Israel in Samaria the seventeenth year of Johoshaphat king of Judah, and reigned two years over Israel. And he did evil in the sight of the Lord, and walked in the way of his father, and in the way of his mother, and in the way of Jeroboam the son of Nebat, who made Israel to sin:" (1 Kings 22:51-42)

"And when Athaliah the mother of Ahazia saw that her son was dead; she arose and destroyed all the seed royal." (2 Kings 11:1)

"Now Jehoram the son of Ahab began to reign over Israel in Samaria the eighteenth year of Jehoshaphat king of Judah, and reigned twelve years. And he wrought evil in the sight of the Lord." (3:1-2)

The Son of Elisabeth and Zecharias

"And it came to pass, that, when Elisabeth heard the salutation of Mary, the babe leaped in her womb; and Elisabeth was filled with the Holy Ghost." (Luke 1:41)

"As it is written in the prophets, Behold, I send my messenger before thy face, which shall prepare thy way before thee. The voice of one crying in the wilderness, Prepare ye the way of the Lord, make his paths

straight. John did baptize in the wilderness, and preach the baptism of repentance for the remission of sins. And there went out unto him all the land of Judea, and they of Jerusalem, and were all baptized of him in the river of Jordan, confessing their sins." (Mark 1:2-5)

Salome's Sons

"And going on from thence, he saw other two brethren, James the son of Zebedee, and John his brother, in a ship with Zebedee their father, mending their nets; and he called them. And they immediately left the ship and their father, and followed him." (Matthew 4:21-22)

"Then came to him the mother of Zebedee's children with her sons, worshipping him, and desiring a certain thing of him. And he said unto her, What wilt thou? She saith unto him, Grant that these my two sons may sit, the one on thy right hand, and the other on the left, in thy kingdom. But Jesus answered and said, Ye know not what ye ask..." (Matthew 20:20-22)

"Now there stood by the cross of Jesus his mother, and his mother's sister, Mary the wife of Cleophas, and Mary Magdalene. When Jesus therefore saw his mother, and the disciple standing by, whom he loved, he saith unto his mother, Woman, behold thy son! Then saith he to the disciple, Behold thy mother! And from that hour that disciple took her unto his own home." (John 19:25-27)

"Now about that time Herod the king stretched forth his hands to vex certain of the church. And he killed

> *James the brother of John with the sword." (Acts 12:1-2)*

1. The Children of Jacob (Genesis 25:29-34; 27:1-29; 29:29, 32-35; 30:3-8, 9-13, 20; 35:22-25; 37:17-30)

Jacob bore children by several women, as he progressed through various stages of his life. He seems to have passed on different values, at different times, many of which were contradictory.

a. Who were Jacob and Rachel's sons? (Genesis 29:32, 33, 34, 35; 30:6, 20; 35:25) Who did they later become? (32:28)

b. How was Jacob's history similar to that of his older sons? (25:29-34; 27:1-29; 37:17-30) What negative attitudes might some of his older sons have picked up from Jacob, earlier in his life? (29:29; 30:3-8, 9-13; 35:22)

c. How were Jacob's and Joseph's histories similar? (25:21-28; 37:3-5) What values might Joseph have picked up from his father, later in his father's life? (28:10-16; 37:3-9)

d. What attitudes might the various children have picked up from Rachel and Leah? (35:22-26; 29:6-23; 31:3-4, 14-16, 25-27, 33-35)

e. How did the Lord manage to unify this complex family? (42, 43)

f. SUMMARY QUESTION: What does the story of Jacob, his wives, and his children demonstrate about how values are passed from parent to child? Compare and contrast this family with African American families of today.

2. The Children of Jochebed and Amram (Exodus 1; 2:1-13; 4:14-15, 21-22; 6:20; 7:10-12; 15:20-21; Numbers 12:1-2; 26:59)

Living under oppression, Jochebed and Amram taught their children to survive and have faith in God.

a. Into what environment were Jochebed, Amram and their family born? (Exodus 1)

b. Who were Jochebed's and Amram's children? (2:1-2; 6:20; Numbers 26:59)

c. Describe the involvement of Jochebed with her children, while living under oppression. (Exodus 2:1-10)

d. Describe both the negative and positive values that Jochabed may have transmitted to her children. (2:7-13; 4:14-15; 15:20-21; Numbers 12:1-2)

e. What role did Moses eventually play in the lives of the Children of Israel? (Exodus 4:21-22) What role did Aaron play? (4:14-15; 7:10-12) What role did Miriam play? (15:20-2)

f. SUMMARY QUESTION: Draw parallels between the above family and Black families, living under oppression, at various points throughout Black history. What values have Black parents passed onto their children?

3. The Children of Ahab and Jezebel (1 Kings 16:29-33; 22:51-53; 2 Kings 1:1, 17; 3:1-2; 9:7; 11:1; 2 Chronicles 21:6; 22:2, 3)

Ahab and Jezebel stand out as parents who transmitted negative attitudes and values to their children.

a. Who were Ahab and Jezebel, and what type of character did they have? (1 Kings 16:29-33)

b. What impact did Jezebel have on Israel? (16:31-32; 2 Kings 9:7)

c. Who were Ahab and Jezebel's children? (2 Chronicles 21:6; 1 Kings 22:51-53; 2 Kings 1:17; 3:1)

d. What values did Ahab and Jezebel display before their children? (1 Kings 16:29-33; 21:7-14)

e. How did their children "turn out"? (2 Chronicles 22:2, 3; 2 Kings 11:1; 1 Kings 22:51-53; 2 Kings 1:1; 3:1-2)

f. SUMMARY QUESTION: Draw parallels between the family of Ahab and Jezebel and modern families. Are there examples of evil being passed from one generation to the next? Who can break the cycle? (John 3:16)

4. The Son of Elisabeth and Zecharias (Luke 1:1-19, 41-80; Isaiah 40:3; Malachi 3:1; Matthew 11:10; Mark 1:2-5; John 1:15-34)

Elisabeth and Zecharias seem to have transmitted the values that helped John the Baptist recognize the important role that he would play in the world.

a. Who were Elisabeth and Zecharias? (Luke 1:5-19)

b. How did it become known to Elisabeth and Zecharias that their son would play a special role in the world? (1:1-17, 41-45)

c. What prophecies foretold John's important role in the world? (Isaiah 40:3; Malachi 3:1; Matthew 11:10)

d. What indication is there that Elisabeth and Zecharias probably helped little John discover who he was? (Luke 1:41-80) What values must they have transmitted to him?

e. What was the significance of John the Baptist's life? (Mark 1:2-5; John 1:15-34)

f. SUMMARY QUESTION: Recall from African American history parents of people who have played a major role in Black history. Draw parallels between them and Elisabeth and Zecharias. What values did they transmit to their children?

5. The Sons of Salome and Zebedee (Matthew 27:56; 4:21-22; 20:20-28; 10:2; 17:1; 26:37)

As parents of apostles, Salome and Zebedee had a quiet but strong presence in the lives of their sons.

a. Who were Salome and Zebedee, and who were their sons? (Matthew 27:56; 4:21; Mark 1:19, 20; 15:40)

b. How involved was Salome with Jesus and the ministry of her sons? (Mark 15:40)

c. What values, good and bad, might Zebedee and Salome have transmitted to their sons? (Matthew 4:21-22; 20:20-28)

d. What role did John eventually play in the early church? (Acts 3:1; 4:3; 8:14; 15:6, 13; Galatians 2:9; John 21:24; Revelation 1:4)

e. In what sense was James an "eyewitness" to Jesus' ministry? (Matthew 10:2; 17:1; 26:37; Acts 1:13; Mark 5:37; 14:33; Acts 12:2)

f. SUMMARY QUESTION: In order to be a pioneer, a person needs certain values. Could Salome and Zebedee have transmitted these values to their sons? In what ways do African American parents transmit similar values to children who plan to be pioneers in various ways?

6. FAMILY MINISTRY APPLICATION

Outline a program whereby the Black church, acting as an extended family, can teach African American children positive values and discourage them from having negative values.

7. PERSONAL APPLICATION

What values are you teaching your children, nieces, nephews and younger cousins? What values are you teaching children, as a member of the African American extended church family? How can you be a more active force in the lives of the younger generation?

CHAPTER SEVEN

COMMUNICATING AND SOLVING PROBLEMS

**"The tongue kills man and the tongue heals man."
(African Proverb)**

Rebecca was a little surprised when her sister Gloria walked into her kitchen and sat down at the table. Almost immediately tears began to flow. Gloria talked about how long it took her to get the courage to talk about her problem: she didn't enjoy having sex with her husband anymore. This had been going on for years, but lately for some reason, it had become intolerable. "He's not even affectionate," she said. "Most of the time it's wham bam, thank you ma'am, and he is off to sleep. He never hugs me, kisses me, or tells me that he even likes me."

Rebecca asked if she had ever talked to her husband about it. "Once a few years ago, I did," she said. "But it ended up in a big argument. He lost his temper and told me I should understand that he is too tired to be bothered with all of that, after working all day to earn money to take care of the family. He always loses his temper if I try to talk about anything serious."

Gloria went on to say that her husband never really talks to her. One time, though, he told her that he thought it was ridiculous for a Christian woman to hound her husband about sex. He felt that she was rebelling against her role as a woman.

Rebecca was puzzled. She didn't understand why her sister was making such an issue about something that most women she knew took for granted and accepted. She agreed with Gloria's husband. Gloria seemed a little rebellious. She really didn't know what to say to her.

At the root of the issue between Gloria and her husband is not rebellion, but a problem with communication. This type of problem is very common in marriages. Often it surfaces in the form of a sexual problem between the two partners, but that is not the only way it can surface.

This chapter focuses on communication between husband and wife, identifies different types of communication problems, the causes of the problems, and ways that counselors can help couples with such problems to learn to communicate.

What Communication Is. Communication implies a relationship between at least two people in which one person has some effect on the other person. Communication may take place without an exchange of words. Some of the most potent messages are expressed through silence, tears, or gestures. Therefore it is essential that the family learn the meaning of familiar forms of communication utilized by its various members. Just because we may recognize the other person's inability or unwillingness to openly talk at a given moment does not relieve us of the necessity of responding to the unspoken need. The response may be an act of comfort or support, a quiet prayer or patient waiting. An attitude of acceptance of the person is essential if the family is to engage in honest communication. The ability to see and feel through the eyes of another is a valuable asset in communication.

Since communication involves two parties and messages that are shared through words, tones and body language there is the possibility for misunderstanding. Communication skills can be learned that will improve family relationships. These guidelines have assisted many people:

1. Work toward making communication open and honest but avoid hurting people with your tongue. James 3:2 tells us to bridle the tongue which can become a weapon of war.

2. Think before discussing emotional issues so that you will not have regrets later. Taking time to calm down and choose your words with wisdom contributes to clear statements.

3. Rather than use accusatory language (avoid the "you" word), speak instead in "I" language. It places the responsibility for feelings on the right person—yourself—and specifically lets the other person know which of their concrete behaviors led to your reaction. For example: "I feel very disappointed when you do such and such."

4. Take turns speaking without interrupting the other person. Force yourself to restate back to the other person what they just said to ensure accurate listening. The ability to put yourself in the other person's position and see through his eyes always fosters communication. It's called empathizing. Attentive listening is healing; often our people just need to know they are being heard and understood. It tells a people they are not invisible, someone cares.

5. It is easier to accept words of criticism if they are sandwiched between praise and recognition. African American families need to actively express our pleasure in each other's attitudes and actions. Expressing kind, loving words in gentle tones can provide a healing balm to hurting, anxious people.

6. Effective problem solving often involves negotiation. This is possible only if the persons maintain attitudes which are committed to conflict resolution and show willingness to compromise as well as willingness to persist until both sides come out feeling satisfied that they have been heard and that a proposed solution recognizes the need for each to change and be fulfilled.

7. Human beings will err in the process of developing loving relationships and in creating a growth producing home environment. The skills are not learned overnight. Therefore the need for genuine forgiveness is ever present. The ability to forgive—to let go of negative memories, feelings, pain and fears—is a personal battle between the individual holding them and God. They need to be perceived on that level so that spiritual power can be released to heal inner wounds.

A number of different types of communication are useful for families:

1. Romantic Talk

The romance of Solomon with the Shulammite woman found in the Song of Solomon highlights the beautiful role of passion and provides the language and symbolism of romance. Hearing the words of love and affection are especially soothing and appealing to females. Whereas facility in providing this is not an indication of the degree of love and probably is more closely related to early rearing, it does create special meanings for a couple. What can be taught is the identification and expression of feelings to each other. Couples retreats are wonderful opportunities for fostering intimacy and socializing with other Christian couples who are spontaneous and open. Some couples classes provide the arena for discussing gender (male/female) differences in communicating. Approaching these differences with humor and in a nonthreatening manner can lead to insightful adjustment. Sentimental communication along with loving behavior keeps the flame of romance alive in a marriage.

2. Problem Solving/Conflict Resolution Management

Families first have to identify the problem before a strategy can be devised to solve it. Chapter nine offers an approach to dealing with stress and crises. Before utilizing those techniques agreement on the issues facing the family group requires the art of listening to each other.

Genuine listening is healing because it means suspending our own interests and being with the person attentively. While actively listening we don't interrupt or rush to conclusions. If a wife asks her husband to listen and he begins to offer advice, he has not done what was asked. This is also true if a husband wants a wife to listen and she interrupts or completes his sentences. Or, if children share with parents in their own language and parents correct or criticize, then true expression is thwarted.

Just listen! That is the first fundamental response to relieving someone's stress. Knowing one is being heard and understood does not necessarily indicate agreement, just a belief that a person has a right to express his/her point of view.

For example, sexual drives are very potent in men when they are very young, usually reaching a peak around 18-20 years old. With women, it is just the reverse, with women peaking around 40. Sexual drive is subject to fluctuations and influenced by many factors such as state of health, medications, stress and anxiety level. As we move through the life cycle we have to be loving in order to live together. We have to stretch to live together happily, and fulfill one another's needs. God designed men and women, who are very often at different points of development, with different drives and needs at different times. Marital relationships can be very dynamic when partners put the interest and full development of their mate before their own interest and are willing to creatively work to resolve the particular issues they face as a couple.

The resolution of these issues is dependent upon working them out together. Sometimes in the process families discover that they don't have enough answers, information or objectivity. Good problem solving requires accumulating information, identifying options and weighing the advantages and disadvantages of those options. When the family has used all its resources or exhausted things to do trusted friends or spiritual Christians can either offer assistance or refer to appropriate sources. In today's complex world expertise in many areas requires consultation by family members and outside resources. When a family can no longer solve problems professional counseling is called for.

We can minimize stress with our mate in much the same way we would minimize stress with anyone else. We have to reassure them overtly that even though we're growing, they are still important to us. So many men are afraid that, if a woman grows, she will not need them anymore. They ask what place they will have in the wife's life if the wife becomes too independent. This means that, as Christian women growing, we need to keep reassuring them. It may mean cutting out certain things for a while to reassure them until they feel restored and reassured. This is also true for men whose pace of growth exceeds that of their wife.

A part of our Christian responsibility is to encourage growth in our mates as we share along with God their full development. Juggling has to go on. It's difficult. Women are nurturers and men are protectors, therefore each must consciously look for signs of stress in the family and avoid becoming critical. We also must find ways of "feeding" ourselves inwardly. Part of that means not expecting to have all of our needs met through our relationships with our husbands or wives. Unrealistic expectations of our mates has been fueled by the media. Many need only be fulfilled by God.

3. Instruction, Goal Setting, Family Unity

Families Communicating. Couples need to ask themselves how long it has been since the entire family sat down for a long talk. What was the topic of conversation? Who participated? Who actually talked? Who listened? How did the talk session conclude?

One of the problems of our urban life–style is that it often pulls family members apart in different directions. These different daily life experiences provide opportunities for family members to develop new interests, ideas, attitudes and needs. Particularly noticeable within the family may be new beliefs and attitudes that members display that are not shared or understood by other family members. Changes in behavior may be observed without others understanding why these occurred. People have lost touch with each other even though they share the same household.

What can be done to prevent or counteract this potentially deteriorating influence within the family? People must work at maintaining open communication. That means even on days when they return home tired, there should be a willingness to listen to someone else's concerns as well as attempts to share with the group their own feelings. Both kinds of exchanges are necessary periodically for each member if this is to become part of an ongoing climate of sharing within the home. If it is done frequently enough, negative feelings can be dealt with before they become major obstacles, and positive strokes can enhance daily life.

One of the major ingredients for communication is being able to listen, free of prejudging. On the other hand it also demands that a person think about him/herself, in order to sort out and express what s/he is feeling and experiencing.

Family Meetings. We have found that in addition to continually working at maintaining open, supportive family relationships, it is also necessary to set aside regular times for meeting together. This helps you catch up with one another and clear the air. This is a time when everyone's concerns and priorities become the focus of family attention. These discussions may occur around the dinner table, or on a family trip. They are a good substitute for watching television and can be a lot more fun.

What topics need to be addressed in family meetings? Following are some suggestions:

1. Attitudes and beliefs about God, self, others, and life purposes.
2. Family plans (present and future) and special family rituals.
3. Problem–solving strategies for the unique experiences the family faces by virtue of its race, urban existence, family structure, Christian belief, work schedule, etc.

4. Ways of making the family unit work better for all of its members, fun times, dream times.
5. Ways of handling the varied emotions involved in human relationships.
6. Subgroup sharing between father-son, mother-daughter, older brother or sister with younger ones, all of which prepare youth for their adult roles.

Benefits of Family Communication. The positive benefits derived from keeping two-way communication operating within our homes are innumerable. Rather than through lecturing, family members experience what it means to live in loving, cooperative relationships. Communication provides a stable, secure foundation from which the family can move confidently into the world, grounded in their faith. Each person grows as a result of communicating. S/he grows in his/her own life, and in the life of the group. Each person comes to know that s/he has the resources of the others available to him/her when needed.

Then, as inevitable differences occur between people, communication provides a way of helping them tolerate and learn from changes while still maintaining a united, functioning family unit. Ultimately, nuclear family experiences in communication prepare us for fuller participation within the larger family of God.

The Issue of Men Talking. A commonly reported problem voiced by wives is their inability to get their husbands to discuss things with them. The scenario is fairly predictable. An incident occurs when something has gone wrong, perhaps at work. The husband comes home and will say nothing. In this situation a wife can pressure the husband, forget the matter, ignore him, or she can accept that he is unable or unwilling to share it, at least for the moment. The latter necessitates a willingness to permit another person to handle his emotions in the manner most natural for him. It means not selfishly imposing one's own needs and style on a mate. The act of true acceptance by one person has the effect of validating another sense of worth.

Timing is important as are creating conditions of readiness. Sometimes people need space. They may need aloneness. They may need to eat; they may need to relax. Husbands and wives must learn each other's patterns and figure out the best time for that person to talk. With men who come from homes where feelings and issues were not discussed, the wife's patience, modeling and timing are especially important for some to learn to share inner feelings. It is sometimes easier to admit and accept help from a wife or husband. This is where the church can help if it has a family ministry. The spouse may need to get their mate to the church and in a situation where people are learning how to trust and communicate. These sessions can provide a setting where without judging or condemning, people skills can be learned and practiced without embarrassment.

The Role of the Church. The church has to equip the home to develop communication skills through facilitating effective communication among the congregation and between leaders and the membership. The church has to help because some families are too wounded to teach themselves. All of us need help with communication at some point in our lives, men and women need to learn each other's needs. We also should accept the responsibility of expressing clearly our needs and wants without expecting people to read our minds.

That's what marriage is all about. It is sharing and receiving. It is loving and being loved. It is helping the other person grow and growing oneself.

Summary. This chapter has focused on communication within marriage and within the family. The issue of differences between men and women in the area of talking was presented. The importance of listening was discussed. The benefits of family communication were presented, along with guidelines for family meetings. The role of the church in helping families learn to communicate also was presented.

The following exercise provides the opportunity to apply the principles covered in this chapter to the study of a biblical family.

BIBLE FAMILIES

INSTRUCTIONS: Following are exercises which allow you to apply the principles covered in this chapter to the analysis of a biblical family. The first five exercises consist of "fill-in-the-blank" discovery questions. The sixth exercise allows you to apply the principles to a church–based family ministry. The seventh exercise is a personal application.

Esther and Ahasuerus

"And all the king's servants, that were in the king's gate, bowed and reverenced Haman: for the king had so commanded concerning him. But Mordecia bowed not, nor did him reverence." (Esther 3:2)

"And when Haman saw that Mordecai bowed not, nor did him reverence, then was Haman full of wrath." (3:5)

"...Wherefore Haman sought to destroy all the Jews that were throughout the whole kingdom of Ahasuerus, even the people of Mordecai."(3:6)

"So Esther's maids and her chamberlains came and told it her. Then the queen was exceedingly grieved..."(4:4)

"And the king said again unto Esther on the second day at the banquet of wine, What is thy petition, queen Esther? and it shall be granted thee..."(7:2)

"Then Esther the queen answered and said, If I have found favour in thy sight, O king, and if it please the king, let my life be given me at my petition, and my people at my request: For we are sold,

I and my people, to be destroyed, to be slain, and to perish..."(7:3-4)

"Then the king Ahasuerus answered and said unto Esther the queen, Who is he, and where is he, that dost presume in his heart to do so?" (7:5)

"and Haman stood up to make request for his life to Esther the queen; for he saw that there was evil determined against him by the king." (7:7)

"Then the king said, Hang him thereon." (7:9)

"So they hanged Haman on the gallows that he had prepared for Mordecai..." (7:10)

1. Open and Honest Communication (Esther 1:1-22; 2:1-8, 10, 12-23; 3:5-6; 4:4, 10-15; 7:2-10; 8:1-7, 11; 9:2, 5, 12, 23-26)

Esther stood out among women in her openness and honesty.

a. Under what circumstances did Esther meet Ahasuerus? (Esther 1:1, 3, 10, 22; 2:1-8)

b. What type person was Ahasuerus? (1:1-22; 2:21-23)

c. How did Esther communicate with Ahasuerus? (2:12-23)

d. Was Esther fair in the way she dealt with the fact that she was Jewish? (2:10, 18-20; 3:5-6; 4:4, 10-15; 7:2-6)

e. What was the outcome of Esther's honesty? (7:7-10; 8:1-7, 11; 9:2, 5, 12, 23-26)

f. SUMMARY QUESTION: What principles about honesty and openness can be learned from the story Esther and Ahasuerus? How do they apply to modern couples today?

2. The Art of Timing (Esther 1:1-3, 10:13; 15-21; 4:9-11; 5:1-15; 7:1-10; 8:1-7; 9:1, 2, 5-16)

There is a time and a place for communication.

a. What risks was Esther taking in going against a rule of the king? (1:1-3, 10-13, 15-21; 4:9-11)

b. What steps did Esther take to prepare the king to listen to her? (5:1-5; 7:3-4)

c. How did Esther space her communications? (5:3-8; 7:1-10; 8:1-7; 9:1, 2, 5-16)

d. How important was the setting in which Esther's communication took place? (5:3-8; 7:1-10; 8:1-7; 9:1, 2, 5-16)

e. How important was Ahasuerus' emotional state for communication to take place? (5:3-8; 7:1-10; 8:1-7; 9:1, 2, 5-16)

f. SUMMARY QUESTION: What principles about timing can be learned from the marriage of Esther and Ahasuerus? How can they be applied to marriage today?

3. Assertiveness (Esther 2:21-23; 4:1-16; 5:1-6; 7:1-10; 9:13-25)

Being open and honest involves being assertive.

a. Explain the ways in which Esther demonstrated that she was not a passive woman. (2:21-23)

b. Explain other ways in which Esther demonstrated that she was not a passive woman. (4:1-16)

c. Explain another way in which Esther demonstrated that she was not a passive woman. (5:1-6)

d. Explain another way in which Esther demonstrated that she was not a passive woman. (7:1-10)

e. Explain yet another way in which Esther demonstrated that she was not a passive woman. (9:13-25)

f. SUMMARY QUESTION: What principle about assertiveness can be learned from the marriage of Esther and Ahasuerus? How can they be applied to modern marriages?

4. Power (Esther 2:1-4, 8, 16-19, 21-23; 5:1-8, 12; 7:1-10; 8:1-4; 9:12-14, 25-26, 29-32)

Esther moved from a relatively powerless to a powerful position in her relationship to Ahasuerus.

a. At the beginning of her relationship with Ahasuerus, did

Esther have much power? Explain. (2:1-4, 8, 16-19)

b. How did Esther gain power in her relationship with Ahasuerus? (2:21-23; 5:1-3)

c. What decision-making power was eventually delegated to Esther? (5:3-8, 12; 7:1-10)

d. How did Esther become a partner in power with the king? (8:1-4; 9:12-14, 25-26, 29-32)

e. Who is the source of power in human relationships? (Matthew 28:18; John 1:12; Ephesians 1:18-23; Acts 1:8)

f. SUMMARY QUESTION: What principles about power in relationships can be learned from the marriage of Esther and Ahasuerus? How can this be applied to modern marriage?

5. God's Interventions (Esther 2:10, 21-23; 3:1-9; 4:1, 21-23; 6:1-11; 7:2-10; 8:4-7; 9:3, 4)

God works behind the scenes to build strong marriages.

a. How did the Lord pave the way for Esther to earn Ahasuerus' respect? (Esther 2:21-23)

b. How did the Lord remove the threat of anti-Semitism that surrounded their marriage? (2:10; 3:1-9; 4:1; 7:2-10; 8:4-7)

c. How did the Lord work in Esther's and Ahasuerus' extended family? (2:21-23; 6:1-11; 9:3, 4)

d. How did the Lord get rid of Esther's enemies?

e. How did the Lord use the marriage of Esther and Ahasuerus to keep the Jews from being exterminated?

f. SUMMARY QUESTION: What principles can be learned from Esther and Ahasuerus about God's interventions in marriages?

6. FAMILY MINISTRY APPLICATION

Design a seminar for married couples that teaches the principles presented in this chapter and in the study of biblical families. What would be the objective? What content would be taught? When and where would it be presented?

7. PERSONAL APPLICATION

If you are married, how can you use the principles from this chapter to strengthen your marriage? If you are single, how can you use these principles to relate to members of the opposite sex?

CHAPTER EIGHT

DEVELOPMENTAL CHANGES IN FAMILY LIFE

"The child looks everywhere and often sees nought; but the old man, sitting on the ground, sees everything." (African Proverb)

It was the first fight for Bea and Dan in years. It happened one Monday afternoon, about three weeks after Dan retired from his job at the post office. Bea was sitting on the couch, watching "All My Children," when Dan suddenly walked over to the television and changed the channel to a baseball game. "Go get me some chicken," he said as he sat beside Bea on the couch.

"Now, wait a minute!" Bea said. "I was watching my program and you turned it off."

"Yeah, but I want to watch the baseball game," Dan said matter-of-factly. "Hurry up and get my chicken. Lunch should have been ready hours ago. What's wrong with you lately?"

As Bea sat staring at Dan, she could feel tears filling her eyes. "Ever since he's been home, things have been a mess," she thought.

Later she told her best friend of 30 years, "I can't look at my soaps, I can't even think. All he wants me to do is bring him this, bring him that and clean up after him. It wasn't so bad when he was working. I didn't mind doing it for a few hours at the end of each day. Now it's an all-day stretch. I wish the kids were still here so I would have something to do other than look at him all day."

Bea and Dan have just entered the retirement years of their marriage. No doubt, if they were to reflect on the earlier stages of their marriage, they would recall that each stage of marriage brought with it different challenges, different needs for communication, and different adjustments. There are some fairly standard stages of married life. Once a person understands these stages, a person can anticipate the changes that each stage brings, and then prepare to adjust to each stage.

One of the reasons so many marriages fail today is that couples do not consider or plan for this aspect of married life. From the very beginning, they start their relationships with the attitude, "I hope we'll always feel just as we do today." Many even dream that such feelings will last, perhaps even as long as the retirement years. That is, forever! However, the wedding day presents a very romanticized view of married life. As time passes and feelings change, so many couples believe they have fallen out of love and many want to dissolve the marriage. However, in most cases just changing marital partners will not solve the problem.

A more realistic view of marriage is one in which we accept the fact that feelings fluctuate and that changes will occur in the relationship. Although feelings are subject to change, it does not imply that the basic commitment to God and to each other changes. For it is personal commitment to God through Jesus Christ and commitment to family members and the purpose of family that become the basis for Christian family life. A marriage requires effort and work to keep it fresh and meaningful for the individuals involved. Therefore we should expect periodically to examine the relationship and reshape it in light of current needs.

This chapter examines the stages through which a typical marriage progresses, from initial attraction to the senior years. It presents guidelines for preparing and adjusting to these phases of the life cycle.

Initial Attraction. Most of the important decisions we're going to make in life are probably greatly influenced by forces that are unconscious. When we are not aware of them, it is difficult to logically and rationally work them out. Why is it that, among the thousands of people eligible in terms of age when you married, you were attracted to just a few or to one in particular. One of the reasons is there were some unconscious factors that influenced you.

Those unconscious factors are related to childhood and early experiences in building relationships. The first experience was with parents. That was the first psychological lesson we had to learn. Issues, at that time, revolved around questions of, "How do I survive in this family? How do I survive in this setting as a child? What are these people like? What is Mom like? What is Dad like?" They gave us the prototypes of human relationships. We learned that, no matter how good they were, they were not perfect. As we grew up and developed our personalities, we became shaped by those people and the settings and circumstances of our lives. We learned there was a part of ourselves and our behaviors that got rewarded, encouraged and reinforced. However, there were other parts of ourselves that got suppressed and pushed to the unconscious level.

If we expressed it, people didn't like it. It didn't get approval and wasn't encouraged. However it didn't go away. It just got pushed out of our conscious minds. It then became a part of our dreams. It sometimes even became a part of our fantasies. It became a part of our "I wish I could," if ever the chance would come.

Then there is the part of us that is kind of a mask. It developed in order to get along, to be Daddy's girl, or Mama's girl, or Grandma's little girl. Our "mask" incorporated some of

151

what we were really like, but a great deal of what others expected of us as well. As adults, whether we're 20, 80 or 85, in each of us there are still parts of ourselves that never were fully realized. Parts of ourselves were lost, or never were fully developed.

Our moms and dads could not fully satisfy these parts because they were human. They had limitations. When we came here as little babies we wanted everything all the time. So no matter how good they were there was no way our parents could completely fulfill all of our needs. One obvious example is that we came really needing a perfect spiritual relationship with God. Parents could not fulfill this need for us.

Many people reach adulthood still looking for human substitutes for a personal relationship with God. They long for someone of the opposite sex to make them happy, secure and complete. No one can do that for another person.

Then we reach the age of attraction and marriage, not having been completely satisfied by our parents, and wanting a perfect human relationship. The false self we developed grows so that we aren't even aware of it. This is all the more complicated by the fact that our society promotes romantic love and physical attributes as a basis for marriage. We idealized our future mates seeing only the parts of them that we want to see.

What appears to happen is that when we are attracted to a person, part of the mystery of the attraction is that somehow we are attracted to people who have within themselves some of both the positive and negative traits of our parents. Now what attracts are positive traits. They may not be in the same form; they could be disguised. It would be too anxiety-provoking for us, if it were obvious. There's something about the person to whom we are attracted that makes him/her similar to our parents. What we tend not to see are the negative tendencies that may surface after marriage.

Generally we don't recognize the negatives they have that were also shared by our parents. Part of what we admired about our parents was their physical appearance. Therefore part of the attraction to a mate has to do with physical attraction. Their beauty is so suggestive. The physical appearance that we associate in the deep recesses of our mind with someone who cares, and with someone who belongs to us. We think of those warm feelings that were conjured up as a result.

The Honeymoon Period. During the honeymoon period, romantic feelings prevail. It is an extension of courtship and a period of new discoveries. Regardless of how well you think you know each other during courtship, marriage will bring new discoveries. Expectations are generally unrealistically high. We want them to make up for all that others have not given us and what we haven't been able to give ourselves.

The Early Years. Once the honeymoon period wanes, the more realistic early years of marriage begin. These are some of the most hazardous years. During this time couples begin to really get to know one another. At this time, more of the total self becomes revealed. After we move through the stage of romantic love, we become aware that this mate of ours also has some negative traits. These negative traits may not be so bad because we are adults and mature enough to realize that. Differences in daily habits, ways of solving problems, and choice of friends, all require good communication and negotiation. However, differences in values can cause major conflicts.

This also is the period of economic pressures as we establish a new household. The basic habits of relating are formed during this period. Ways of communicating, showing affection, respect, resolving differences, going to church, etc., are all instituted during this time. A joined life-style contributed to by two different people must be created.

The Birth of Children. The birth of children ushers the family into a new phase. As the family circle enlarges, life becomes more complex with increasing demands. Ideals about mother/father roles are tested during this period. Long hours of work, child care, and career development require more compromises and more cooperation within the family. Marriage becomes complex as husband and wife must continue to respond to one another's needs, growth and changes. However, while continually adjusting, they also must work together as parents to cope with the ever-changing needs of their children and the new life situation the children bring. There is less time for self and spouse. Most arguments during this period center around money and child rearing issues.

Emptying the Nest. When the children grow up and leave home, yet another phase of marriage begins. In some instances these years can also become wrought with conflict. This is particularly true if a couple's lives and affections have been centered around the children exclusively. Sometimes husbands and wives have neglected their relationship in working to become good parents. It is also true when the marriage has a history of one or the other partners being taken for granted. A crisis can also occur when new middle-aged needs are being felt by one or both partners. Men and women may have their own unique ways of experiencing a mid-life crisis.

After the age of 50 men generally become more comfortable with their emotions and dependency needs. Whereas women in this phase, after nurturing children, are eager for personal growth, independence and power.

If parents are overly involved in the lives of their adult children, they may fail to make the best decisions for their life as a couple. Many Black families find that grandparenting is filled with both unexpected demands and rewards as they assist their children. Increasingly adult children, often accompanied with their young, are returning home due to economic conditions. Traditionally we have always had more multi-generational homes, but responsibilities and roles do have to be clearly spelled out. These also may become the "sandwich" years, when we are torn between assisting our children in getting established and caring for our own parents.

In these cases, it will be necessary to reshape the marital **relationship so that it provides more mutual satisfaction. It will** require a rekindling of romance and the development of new opportunities for growth and service to one another.

The Senior Years. Following the period of emptying the nest come the senior years. These years may be comfortable and harmonious or disruptive, depending on how the previous life cycles were managed. Retired people who remain active and productive adjust more successfully.

A fresh look at how the couple relates to one another must be taken at this stage. An effort must be made to avoid excessive criticism and nagging. These years are best approached with conscious, realistic plans. Often illness, dependence or death demand a complete change in family life. Health conditions greatly influence the quality of life experienced during these years. Since health risks are so prevalent among African American men, unlike other Americans their life expectancy is not increasing. Therefore only a small percentage of Black couples have the opportunity to build a relationship of over 40 or 50 years that has weathered storms, overcome obstacles and celebrated many victories. What an incentive for women to help husbands watch their diet, stress level and life-style.

These cycles are less dramatic in childless families. However, throughout the life cycle, childless families will need to work harder at stimulating their marriage. The cycles become more hazardous when divorce and death occur early in the family life.

Adjusting to One Another. Adjustments are necessary in every marriage. However, some marriages require more profound adaptations than others. Adaptability refers to the person's capacity to change his roles, attitudes, and behavior in order to adjust to those of another person or to a new situation.

Adjustments are easier to make when both parties come from similar home environments and share similar values and experiences. However no two people enter marriage with identical values, ideals and experiences. The differences in background begin to appear as soon as the husband and wife undertake their new roles.

One of the reasons we have so many problems in marriage, is that we don't know our areas of vulnerability. We don't realize the relationship between power and our own vulnerability. This is particularly true among people who have a high level of responsibility. It seems that God gives us responsibility and the more He enriches our ministries, the more vulnerable we become.

Therefore we need to know the specific areas of our temptation. We need to be aware of our weaknesses so that we can keep vigilant watch over those areas. We must do this so that we make very specific provisions for protecting those areas of temptation. Sexual temptation is a common means for corrupting. We need prayer mentors. We need people with whom we can take our masks off and uncover our areas of weakness. Then we must observe ourselves and our behavior in order to see if we are getting off track. Leaders should be accountable in their marriages to be examples of Christ-like behavior.

There is an exercise which couples can complete at almost any stage of the life cycle. This exercise can be the foundation for rediscovering oneself and understanding more about one's partner. First of all, each partner takes several sheets of paper. One is labeled with the name of the person's mate, one with the name of the person's father, one with the name of the person's mother, and one with the person's name. Then two columns are created on each sheet. Above the first columns, write "Good traits". Above the second columns, write "Bad traits". Do this for each sheet.

Then, on each sheet list the good and bad traits of the person whose name the sheet bears, in the respective columns for those traits. Then compare each sheet with the sheet which outlines the person's own good and bad traits. Are there similarities and differences? Do you see the point that is being made?

Most people will recognize a commonality between the list for their parents and for themselves. They may also find similarities between the list for their spouse and the list for their parents. In doing this exercise, what you have uncovered is an unconscious factor in marriage choice. This concept has been stressed in many words by many people. Dr. Hendricks has discussed it in his book *Getting the Love You Want* which deals with the issue of why we are attracted to particular people.

We live in a world where both secular and Christian thought often centers around marrying the right person. Many people will use this as the rationale for their failed marriage: "They didn't marry the right person. It couldn't have worked. We were not compatible, we weren't well suited." Many divorcees use incompatibility, or irreconcilable differences, as the explanation. Part of what Dr. Hendricks helps them see is why we are attracted to certain people, and why we married as well as why we experienced conflict with spouses.

Guidelines for Counseling Couples Through the Life Cycle. Counselors should alert couples to the fact that some of the most common marital problems surface when partners allow themselves to become too self-centered or excessively critical of one another. Selfishness, the very root of the "unredeemed human" effectively prevents deep involvement and adaptation to anyone.

Like any living thing, both the marriage and the family require daily nourishment and a daily development of strategies for coping with major changes. The cultivation of love and compatibility paves the way for successful handling of the crises stages. This love expresses itself in the desire to be helpful and understanding of one another. When these principles of learning, love and growth are practiced in relationship to God and family members, times of major adaptation can be met with greater inner strength and security.

With these characteristics, family members can become more sympathetic and can better accept the work, time and problem-solving techniques required to make major adaptations.

Following is a list of principles which a counselor can provide couples to be practiced as they progress through the cycles of life:

1. Expect changes in feelings so don't make major decisions based just on emotions.
2. Learn to ask forgiveness and forgive one another.
3. To ward off boredom, periodically add something new to life's routine.
4. Exchange affection in thoughtful ways.
5. Maintain a physical relationship.
6. Take vacations together. Have frequent fun times together.
7. End your days on a positive note.
8. As a team, constantly improve the spiritual, intellectual and physical environment of your home.
9. Cultivate a good sense of humor.
10. Avoid blaming one another for shortcomings.
11. Try to keep growing together throughout the marriage.
12. Pray and study the Scriptures together, as a family.

In addition to the above principles there are other resources that the counselor can use while counseling couples. The first resource is God. God becomes a resource as we allow Him to control our lives. According to 1 Corinthians 3, our relationship with God progresses through stages, just as a marriage does. We develop in our relationship with God in the same way that new-born babies grow to spiritual maturity.

As we deepen our relationship with God, we learn to adapt to our own inner changes and to one another. Genuine communion with God always results in changed relationships with people.

Summary. This chapter has presented an overview of stages through which a typical marriage progresses, including: the initial attraction, the honeymoon period, the early years, the birth of children, emptying the nest, and the senior years. Principles for adjusting to each stage were discussed, and guidelines for counseling couples through various stages of the life cycle were also presented.

Following is an exercise which provides the opportunity to apply principles covered in this chapter to the study of a biblical family.

BIBLE FAMILIES

INSTRUCTIONS: The following exercise allows you to apply the principles from this chapter to the study of a biblical family. The first five exercises consist of five "fill-in-the-blank" discovery questions. The sixth exercise allows you to apply the principles to a church-based family ministry. The seventh exercise allows for personal application.

Isaac and Rebekah

"And it came to pass, before he had done speaking, that, behold, Rebekah came out, who was born to Bethuel, son of Milcah, the wife of Nahor, Abraham's brother, with her pitcher upon her shoulder. And the damsel was very fair to look upon, a virgin, neither had any man known her: and she went down to the well, and filled her pitcher, and came up." (Genesis 24:15-16)

"And they called Rebekah, and said unto her, Wilt thou go with this man? And she said, I will go. And they sent away Rebekah their sister, and her nurse, and Abraham's servant, and his men." (24:58-69)

"And Rebekah lifted up her eyes, and when she saw Isaac, she lighted off the camel. For she had said unto the servant, What man is this that walketh in the field to meet us? And the servant had said, It is my master: therefore she took a veil, and covered herself. And Isaac brought her into his mother Sarah's tent, and took Rebekah, and she became his wife; and he loved her: and Isaac was comforted after his mother's death." (24:64-65, 67)

1. Initial Attraction (Genesis 12:10, 20; 24:15-16; 26:1-11)

Initial attraction is often based on similarities between the object of one's affections and one's parents.

a. What is one way in which Sarah (Isaac's mother) and Rebekah, his wife were similar? (Genesis 12:10, 20; 24:15-16; 26:1-11)

b. What is one trait, other than physical, that made Rebekah suitable for Isaac? (24:5-8)

c. What is another trait that made Rebekah suitable for Isaac? (24:5-8)

d. What evidence is there that the Lord was in control of the initial meeting between Isaac and Rebekah? (24:12-15)

e. What evidence is there that Rebekah reminded Isaac of his mother? (24:67)

f. SUMMARY QUESTION: Make a list of the factors that became important in the matching of Isaac and Rebekah. Are these factors still considered during dating today? Are they still important? Explain.

2. The Early Years (1 Samuel 1:5-6; Luke 1:6-7, 24-25)

The first twenty years of the marriage of Isaac and Rebekah were disturbed by Rebekah's barrenness.

a. How did Jews treat women who were barren? (1 Samuel 1:5-6; Luke 1:6-7, 24-25)

b. Of what was barrenness seen as a result? (Isaiah 47:9; Leviticus 20:20, 21)

c. How common was barrenness? (Genesis 11:30; 25:21; 29:31; Judges 13:2, 3; Luke 1:7, 36)

d. What was a common practice that resulted from anxiety over barrenness? (Genesis 16:2)

e. How might barrenness have affected the marriage of Isaac and Rebekah? (25:21)

f. SUMMARY QUESTION: The lack of children is one problem that African American couples could face, early in marriage. What are some other forms of "barrenness"?

3. The Birth of Children (Genesis 25:22-28)

When children enter a marriage, the family structure and dynamics change.

a. What was Rebekah's pregnancy like? (25:22-23)

b. How were Esau and Jacob different? (25:24-25)

c. How did the parents, Isaac and Rebekah, respond to the differences in their children? (25:28) In what ways might Rebekah's response to Jacob have been a result of events in her childhood? (28:5; 24:15, 29)

d. How may the favoritism of the parents have affected the relationship between the two children? (25:29-34)

e. In what type environment did Jacob and Esau grow up? (26:1-22)

f. SUMMARY QUESTION: Are there ways in which African American parents of the past or present have "played favorites" among their children, based on physical appearances and other external features? How might this "favoritism" have affected relationships between children?

4. Emptying the Nest (Genesis 25:21-28; 27:1-10, 21-38; 28:1-4)

When children grow up and are at a point of leaving home, this sometimes introduces conflict into the family and the marriage of the parents.

a. At what point in the marriage of Isaac and Rebekah did Jacob and Esau prepare to leave home? (27:1; 28:1-4)

b. What basic conflict between Isaac and Rebekah reached a new height at the point when the children were ready to leave home? (25:21-28; 27:1-10)

c. In what ways does Rebekah's behavior reflect an intensity of feelings that may have spilled over from her childhood?

(25:27-28)

d. Describe the problems that escalated between various members of Isaac's family as the children prepared to leave the nest. (27:6-38, 41-46)

e. How did problems between Jacob and Esau, at the point when they were leaving their parents' nest, affect future generations? (27:36-46; 28:1-9; 36:1-43; 48:20-22; 1 Chronicles 5:1-2)

f. SUMMARY QUESTION: Can certain principles be drawn from Isaac's and Rebekah's life, when their children prepared to leave the nest? How do these relate to African American families today?

5. The Senior Years (Genesis 22:23; 25:28; 26:34-38; 28:6-9; 29:9-30; 31:1-23; 32; 30:25-43; 36:1-7; 37:1-4, 13, 14, 18, 23-24; 35:22; 48:20-22; 49:1-28; 1 Chronicles 5:1-2)

In the senior years, often unresolved conflicts with children express themselves through grandchildren.

a. What was the probable relationship between Isaac, Rebekah and the children of Esau? (Genesis 26:34-38; 28:6-9; 36:1-7)

b. How did the "favoritism" of Isaac and Rebekah influence Jacob's relationship with his children? (25:28; 29:32; 37:1-4; 48:20-22; 1 Chronicles 5:1-2)

c. How might the pattern of "favoritism" throughout Isaac's and Rebekah's extended family network have shaped the personalities of their grandchildren? (Genesis 37:1-4, 13-14, 18, 23-24; 35:22; 49:1-28)

d. How might conflicts on Rebekah's side of the family have affected their extended family network? (22:23; 28:6; 29:9-30; 30:25-43; 31:1-23; 26:34-35; 36:1-2)

e. Describe how the Lord brought various warring factions of Isaac's and Rebekah's extended family together. (31:1-55; 33:1-20)

f. SUMMARY QUESTION: What principles about grandparent-

162

ing can be drawn from Isaac's and Rebekah's marriage and taught to newlyweds? How do these principles apply to developing marriages today?

6. FAMILY MINISTRY APPLICATION

Using the contents of this chapter and the story of Isaac and Rebekah as guides, make a list of topics for a church-based seminar on parenting, grandparenting and honesty in marriage.

7. PERSONAL APPLICATION

Are there any similarities between the marriage and extended family of Isaac and Rebekah and your family? Are there any lessons that can be drawn from their lives and then applied to families today?

CHAPTER NINE

HANDLING CRISIS AND STRESS

"If a string of pearls breaks in the presence of grown-up people, nothing is lost." (African Proverb)

It was lunchtime, and Joe and Bart were heading toward Smitty's where they usually ate lunch. While they were waiting for their usual hamburgers and fries, Bart told Joe that he had been having pains in his chest lately. He started having them shortly after he heard there might be a layoff at the plant where they worked.

"Are you and Jeanette getting along now?" Joe asked.

"Naw, man, we had a big fight last night," Bart said. "He keeps nagging me about spending more time with Mickey."

"Did you ever find out if Mickey joined that gang?" Joe asked.

"Naw, man. I ain't got time for that stuff. I look at it like this, man. I work every day to bring home the bacon. It's her job to see after the kids, you know what I'm sayin'?"

"Is she still having trouble on her job?" Joe asked.

"I don't know, man. I haven't talked to her," Bart answered. "I don't have the time. I usually stop over here to Smitty's for a couple of hours after work. By the time I get home, she's already putting the kids to

bed. I just get my dinner off the stove and turn on the set."

"What were you fighting about last night, man?" asked Joe.

"She's always pretending she's sick. Especially since she got pregnant. You know how women try to get out of doing work around the house. She had the nerve to talk about taking a vacation or something. I told her to get off my back. I get sick of her complaining and nagging all of the time."

Bart went on to say that he was going to see the doctor about his chest pains. He thought it might be his nerves. If Jeanette was more of a wife and mother, he told his friend, maybe he wouldn't be having chest pains.

Bart and Jeanette are showing signs of stress. A close examination of the story would reveal a number of stressors being experienced by both Bart and his wife Jeanette. In addition to what may be longstanding sources of stress, the family also appears to be in the throws of a crisis that may occur if either one or both of the partners loses employment. However, Bart seems unaware of the real sources of his or Jeanette's stress.

In order to establish a healthy family life, it is important to know what is causing stress in one's life. At the onset of a crisis, it is also important to understand the nature of crisis, the ways in which one typically responds to crisis, and alternative strategies for dealing with a crisis to restore equilibrium to one's life and the lives of one's family members.

This chapter focuses on some of the most common sources of stress in everyday family life. Then it discusses the nature and source of crisis, the effects of crisis on the body and some principles for dealing with stress and crisis.

Common Sources of Stress. The stressors to be discussed in this section are those which have been identified in surveys a cross section of people representing various ethnic and economic backgrounds. The people were asked to name the ten top sources of stress in their lives.

The top three stressors on all lists, whether male or female, single or married, Black or white, had to do with money. Money was the top priority on nearly every list. The next most common stressor was the lack of a mate's willingness to share responsibility for family life. This particular stressor is common in families where women work outside of the home. In counseling, such women often report chronic fatigue. Fatigue accumulates over years of working on a full-time job and handling the primary responsibility for day-to-day parenting.

Next on the list of stressors was insufficient time spent with one's mate. Women complain that they always have to take the lead in arranging times that they share with their husbands. Such women do so much nurturing that, if they are to continue nurturing, they also must be nurtured. They need a situation in which mates share with one another and nurture one another. They do not feel that nurturing should all go one way—from them to their mates and others. Single parents and singles share these concerns along with feelings of loneliness.

Another stressor has to do with insufficient "me" time. People complain that they do not have enough time to be alone or enough time for exercise or recreation.

Another common stressor is guilt about not accomplishing more. This stressor is often reported by women. Such women complain that they should be doing more. Women who do the most often think they should be doing more. Such women set unrealistic expectations for themselves. They can become engaged in too much mothering and nurturing for both children and adults. This often leads to feelings of guilt related to being unable to solve every problem, and being unable to be everything to everyone.

An additional source of stress is the presence of a poor self-image. Often people have low self-esteem. They feel unattractive. They fear how others may see them. All of this produces stress caused by their excessive dependence upon the approval of others.

The Nature of Crisis. A crisis can be defined as any event which changes or challenges the way in which a family has to cope. Crisis situations are episodic throughout the life span. They may occur as one big event, or they may be experienced as a series of small mishaps. In many cases, the person having the crisis experiences it as "the last straw." Perhaps a person has had problems with children, along with ongoing problems with a mate. Then the person loses his/her job. Then s/he feels s/he can't take life anymore.

The signals of the onset of a crisis include: boredom, fatigue, anxiety, a sense of dissatisfaction with old roles, confusion, lack of a clear vision for the future, the inability to complete tasks and/or the loss of interest in life. People in such crisis states often say that it is like being in a tunnel, with very little light. The person feels unable to see the end of the tunnel or a way out of the tunnel, and that leads to despression and despair.

Crises share a number of things in common. This is true whether the crisis originates within an individual or is triggered by some outside event. First there is a perceived sense of loss. The individual feels that something has left his/her life. It may be something which the person didn't really have, but felt that she/he had. Sometimes the sense of loss is only an illusion. It may merely be a perceived loss but is felt just as stronglly as if it were real.

Events Which Trigger Crises. A crisis can originate from a variety of sources. It can originate from within an individual. For example, a female adolescent might discover that she is pregnant. A parent might discover that an adolescent son is a drug user. Perhaps there is a school failure in the family. A mother, father, grandmother or grandfather might discover that they have a terminal illness.

168

A crisis may even erupt when there is a breakdown in interpersonal relationships between family members. For example a husband and wife may discover that what were once little arguments are now large ones which separate them. A father and his son may withdraw from one another or in-laws may have conflict with a daughter-in-law. Sister withdraws from sister and brother from brother. Marital discord, separation and/or divorce are all examples of crises that are due to breakdowns in relationships within families.

A crisis may be precipitated by an outside event, a sudden, unexpected loss of a job, a move to a new city, a move to a new part of the country, an economic reversal or an experience of racism.

Then there are other crises that appear to rise out of a transition between life stages. Adolescence is a time of upheaval and turmoil. It is a time of trying out multiple roles and experiencing rebellion and defiance. It is a search for independence and identity. The mid-life crisis which occurs in the late 30's and 40's is also a transition which may produce a need for change. A mini life crisis occurs in some people in the late 20's.

Examples of losses that are sometimes only illusions of losses include the loss of a friendship that really wasn't a true friendship, the loss of love from a relative or friend which was never really experienced as love, or the loss of a job which one really didn't enjoy.

The experience of stress and crisis associated with these types of losses is difficult to understand, because the real source of stress is sometimes hidden from view. The loss of a job, for example, is more than the loss of a paycheck. It is also the loss of one's identity, a loss in terms of how one organizes and structures one's day, a loss of a sense of importance, a loss of something to do, and the loss of finances in general.

However, most crises are a natural part of life. This is because crises are usually related to the natural stages of growth that occur as life passes through natural transitions. One can expect that throughout life there will be periods of upheaval, plateaus and depressions. To cope with all of this, one has to adjust one's notions about life. However, these natural transitions become much more difficult to handle when one has been conditioned to think of life as remaining the same rather than consisting of periodic changes, shifts, setbacks, and uphill climbs interspersed by temporary experiences of predictability and rest.

Some people approach every transition as a crisis. Moreover, for some people, life seems to be in a chronic state of crisis, with few periods of stability in between. That is why so many people try to order their lives in such a way that they will not have to make changes. They attempt to protect themselves from having to make changes. Today it is very difficult to avoid changing, because we are living in a world characterized by rapid change.

Stress in the Life of a Christian. Some Christians may question whether knowing the Lord makes them immune to feeling the effects of crisis situations. However, it is important for Christians to realize that they, too are vulnerable to crisis. Christians, as well as others, still carry with them a "backpack" from early childhood. The backpack consists of preredemptive experiences—the garbage which often surfaces when undergoing stress.

All people come to adulthood with a unique backpack that is filled with good things and bad things (garbage) from childhood. One type of garbage which Christians often carry is the reaction of getting disturbed and feeling depressed when faced with stress. Another type of garbage is getting sick when things get rough. Another is not following through on various tasks. Yet another type is becoming very critical of other people or withdrawing all together from people.

One needs to examine one's backpack when one is under stress and in crisis. It is going to surface and one must deal with it. The Holy Spirit has been given for the purpose of leading us into all truth, including the truth of self-insight. This is true of Christians and non-Christians.

Crisis in the Lives of African Americans. Crises are experienced by all people, regardless of race or economic background.

However, African Americans and other minorities of color are especially affected by economic and political upheavals. Poor people and minorities must handle the usual patterns of stress in addition to stress related to these upheavals which may greatly affect income, housing and neighborhoods. Therefore, many African Americans are much more prone to being in a constant state of crisis. This fact is reflected in prevalence rates of physical and mental disorder. This reality has certainly had an impact on Black male/female relationships and family life.

The Effects of Crisis on the Body. In a crisis situation, human balance and equilibrium are disturbed. At this time, s/he may become hysterical and emotional and operate out of feelings alone. S/he may panic, act out, and return to habits s/he once conquered, such as drinking, overeating, physical/verbal abuse or abuse of prescription medication. Then such a person might go into depression, if s/he has had a predisposition toward depression.

Some persons in conflict may become physically ill. Certain organs and parts of the body become vulnerable and react to prolonged stress. Some people experience headaches, some get colitis, while others experience backaches, heart pains, and escalations in blood pressure. If a person has arthritis, this condition may worsen. Allergies may become more intense. One of the ways that stress affects the body biochemically is to attack the immune system so that one cannot ward off disease. During stress, our inner resources for healing are not activated as well as when we are not under stress. At these times we become more vulnerable to physical and emotional illnesses.

As a person becomes depressed, there is a retardation in the ability to remember, to think logically and even in motor activities, everything slows down. This becomes a cause of concern. The depressed person recognizes that s/he is not fully in control of him/herself. That is a scary feeling in today's world.

Events that are occurring may be perceived by the person as a threat to his/her basic needs or independence. The loss may be-

171

come associated with a loss of identity and/or with the loss of some ability.

Predicting and Controlling the Effects of Crisis. Some crises can be predicted and some of the emotional effects controlled. First of all, one has to realize that the usual period of a crisis lasts between six and eight weeks. However, that two-three month period can be very intense. As people are really in the throws of the crisis, they usually reach out for help. Most people will try to resolve the problem because holding onto it is too difficult for the body to withstand.

An ounce of prevention is worth much more than a pound of cure. The best method for controlling the effects of a crisis is to understand oneself and one's individual patterns of response in a crisis. An African guide to wisdom tells us to "Know thyself." To do this, one must identify and then systematically and consciously clear out the garbage. We cannot clear out the garbage unless we bring it before the Lord to have it cleansed.

Another way of preventing some of the severe reactions to crisis is by managing stress in one's everyday life on an ongoing basis. Following are some basic principles that one can use to manage stress in everyday life.

Principle #1: Live a Balanced Life. Take time to relax. Being a good steward means taking care of oneself. Taking care of oneself involves taking time to relax. Work actively at building a balanced life which includes work and play, leisure or hobbies, physical, mental, social and spiritual fulfillment.

Principle #2: Deal Realistically with Pain! Black people, at this point in history, must learn how to deal with pain. Pain is just a reality of life. We can use it as a starting point in life. African Americans need to understand the position of Black people in this society and that this position is worsening. Troubles will come from external and internal problems. The American society is protecting the few resources it has left. In order to deal with this reality, Black Americans must develop a realistic perspective of pain. Group efforts to alleviate inequities

172

can relieve pressure and field a sense of hope and contribution.

When things are going well, a person tends to trust his/her own resources, intellect and past experiences. Perhaps times of growth occur most when things are not going too well if we learn how to transform these times through the renewal of our minds (Romans 12). Even though we are not aware of it at the time, growth can happen. It is difficult to reach the point where one grows in the midst of pain. It is a process of transformation.

Principle #3: Accept Limitations as Temporary. As mentioned previously, many mates feel guilty because they believe they are not nurturing their mates enough. Many feel that they themselves should be able to make their husbands or wives relax. However, there really is only so much that one can do for another person. One cannot change another person. One can only be as much as one can and then it is up to the other person. A person should not relinquish all of his/her private time for someone else. One must have time with oneself and with God in order to survive. This time alone is even more important if one is to give to others. Accepting limitations does not imply that one should give up on goals and dreams. Never! They keep us filled with hope. Regroup, analyze what is needed and modify one's plans.

Principle #4: Be Patient with Others, Particularly One's Mate and Family. Often people expect too much of themselves, and they also expect too much of others. This is particularly true when such people deal with their partners. However, to achieve a mutually satisfying family relationship, parents and partners must be willing to explore one another, learn one another, try various strategies for getting along with one another, and be patient. That is what love is all about.

In any given situation, partners must determine which of several possible strategies would be the least stressful. For example, if one's mate objects to the mate going to a health spa for an aerobics class, might it not be less stressful to purchase a recording or videotape, turn it on, and do the exercises at home together? This requires having patience with one's mate while continuing to educate and discover root causes for concern. However, to achieve harmony within the home, it may be necessary for a partner to take such a step temporarily, just because it is the least stressful path to take without making excessive demands on either person.

Principle #5: Seek Professional Help When Needed. Because all people have limitations, families sometimes exhaust their supply of ideas as to how to solve a problem. When this occurs, the family might want to seek outside professional counseling. A variety of types of professional counseling exist. These include one-to-one counseling and group counseling.

Some professional counselors are useful because they can help a client design plans and monitor how the plans will work for six weeks, ten weeks or longer. This type of counseling helps people patiently try a strategy until it produces results. Sometimes people really haven't given themselves enough time. Moreover, when they "quit" too soon, they may be sabotaging their own plans without realizing it.

Outside help and/or counseling can help couples see whether they indeed have tried everything, and it can give them practice in trying new techniques for getting along with one another. Support groups or a circle of trusted friends can be a lifesaver when undergoing stress.

Principle #6: Spiritual/Mental Attitudes. If one is armed with a set of attitudes which are centered on seeking first the kingdom of God, other experiences can be put in place. Black senior citizens most generally report that their major coping strategy has been their faith in God and the joy of their relationships. Daily meditation on the Scriptures prevents as well as reduces stress.

There is also value in relaxing to music, and practicing good nutrition and periodic exercise. How wonderful our lives would be if less of our time were spent sitting and more of our time actively doing.

Summary. This chapter has focused on stress in family life. It has explained the nature of crises which produce stress, and events that trigger crisis. Stress in the lives of Christians and in the lives of African Americans was explored. The effects of stress on the body was presented. Finally principles for predicting and controlling the effects of stress were provided. The following exercise is an opportunity to apply information from this chapter to an analysis of a biblical family.

BIBLE FAMILIES

INSTRUCTIONS: The following exercises allow you to apply the principles drawn from this chapter to an analysis of some biblical families in crisis. The first five exercises consist of five "fill-in-the-blank" questions plus a summary question. The sixth exercise is an opportunity to apply the principles to a church-based family ministry. The seventh exercise allows for personal application.

Abi, Ahaz, and Hezekiah

"Twenty years old was Ahaz when he began to reign, and reigned sixteen years in Jerusalem, and did not that which was right in the sight of the Lord his God, like David his father." (2 Kings 16:2)

"Now it came to pass in the third year of Hoshea son of Elah king of Israel, that Hezekiah the son of Ahaz king of Judah began to reign. Twenty and five years old was he when he began to reign; and he reigned twenty and nine years in Jerusalem. His mother's name also was Abi, the daughter of Zachariah. And he did that which was right in the sight of the Lord, according to all that David his father did." (2 Kings 18:1-3)

175

The Widow and the Oil

"Now there cried a certain woman of the wives of the sons of the prophets unto Elisha, saying, Thy servant my husband is dead; and thou knowest that thy servant did fear the Lord: and the creditor is come to take unto him my two sons to be bondmen. And Elisha said unto her, What shall I do for thee? tell me, what hast thou in the house? And she [Alu] said, Thine handmaid hath not any thing in the house, save a pot of oil. Then he said, Go, borrow thee vessels abroad of all thy neighbours, even empty vessels; borrow not a few. And when thou art come in, thou shalt shut the door upon thee and upon thy sons, and shalt pour out into all those vessels, and thou shalt set aside that which is full." (2 Kings 4:1-4)

"Then she came and told the man of God. And he said, Go, sell the oil, and pay thy debt, and live thou and thy children of the rest." (4:7)

Job and His Wife

"There was a man in the land of Uz, whose name was Job; and that man was perfect and upright, and one that feared God, and eschewed evil. And there was a day when his sons and his daughters were eating and drinking wine in their eldest brother's house: And there came a messenger unto Job, and said, The oxen were plowing, and the asses feeding beside them: And the Sabeans fell upon them, and

176

took them away; yea, they have slain the servants with the edge of the sword; and I only am escaped alone to tell thee. In all this Job sinned not, nor charged God foolishly." (Job 1:1, 13-15, 22)

Jairus' Daughter

"While he spake these things unto them, behold, there came a certain ruler, and worshipped him, saying, My daughter is even now dead: but come and lay thy hand upon her, and she shall live. But when the people were put forth, he went in, and took her by the hand, and the maid arose. And the fame hereof went abroad into all that land." (Matthew 9:18, 25-26)

The Widow of Nain

"And it came to pass the day after, that he went into a city called Nain; and many of his disciples went with him, and much people. Now when he came nigh to the gate of the city, behold, there was a dead man carried out, the only son of his mother, and she was a widow: and much people of the city was with her. And when the Lord saw her, he had compassion on her, and said unto her, Weep not. And he came and touched the bier: and they bare him stood still. And he said, Young man, I say unto thee, Arise. And he that was dead sat up, and began to speak. And he delivered him to his mother." (Luke 7:11-15)

1. The Widow of Nain (Luke 7:11-15)

In the midst of a crisis a single parent reaches out to the Lord.

a. What event triggered the crisis the widow faced? (Luke 7:11-12)

b. What is one of the reasons that loss of the widow's only son was especially traumatic? (Genesis 49:3; Psalm 78:51; Numbers 18:15-17; Deuteronomy 21:15-17)

c. Without a husband or son, how would the widow be supported? (Deuteronomy 14:29; 26:12; 24:19-21; 16:11, 14)

d. How certain could the widow be that the Jewish community at the time of Christ would take care of her? (Acts 7:51-53; Psalm 94:1-6; Ezekiel 22:1-3, 7; Malachi 3:1, 5)

e. What is the evidence that the widow applied Principles #5 & 6 from this chapter to deal with her crisis? (Luke 7:11-17)

f. SUMMARY QUESTION: In what ways is the widow of Nain similar to many modern African American single parents? What can such parents learn from how she handled her crisis?

2. Abi, Ahaz and Hezekiah (2 Chronicles 29:1)

Although Abi (Abijah) faced the daily crises of being married to a wicked husband she managed to raise a son to love the Lord.

a. Who were Abi, Ahaz and Hezekiah? (2 Kings 18:2; 2 Chronicles 29:1; 2 Kings 16:1-2; 18:1-3)

b. Discuss the general spiritual condition of Ahaz, Abi's husband and Hezekiah's father. (2 Kings 16:1-4, 10-19; 2 Chronicles 28:1-4)

c. In what type of environment did Abi raise Hezekiah? (2 Kings 16:2-33; 2 Chronicles 28:1, 5-8)

d. How was Hezekiah different from his father, Ahaz? (2 Kings 15:1-4; 18:1-8)

e. What role did Abi his mother probably play in Hezekiah's upbringing and what does this say about how she handled the crises associated with being married to Ahaz? (2 Kings 18:1-8)

178

f. SUMMARY QUESTION: In what ways is Abi similar to some modern Christian mothers and fathers? What lessons can be learned from her way of handling the crisis of being married to Ahaz?

3. The Widow and the Oil (2 Kings 4:1-7)

This widow handled an economic crisis by reaching out to the Lord in faith.

a. What event triggered a crisis in the widow's life? (2 Kings 4:1-2)

b. Why did the widow fear that creditors would take her son? (Nehemiah 5:1-13; Leviticus 25:39-41; Proverbs 11:15; 17:18)

c. Who was Elisha and what did he represent? (2 Kings 2:1-15; 3:11-15)

d. Describe the ways in which oil was used in trade. (Ezra 3:1, 6-7; Ezekiel 27:16-18; Hosea 12:1)

e. Why was oil so valuable in the culture at the time? (Ezekiel 16:13; Luke 12:35; Isaiah 61:3)

f. SUMMARY QUESTION: What lesson about economic crisis can we learn from this single parent who reached out to the Lord?

4. Jairus' Daughter (Matthew 9:18-25; Mark 5:21-43; Luke 8:41-56)

While others doubted, Jairus had faith that the Lord could heal his daughter.

a. Who was Jairus? (Mark 5:21; Luke 8:41) Who was his daughter? (Luke 8:42)

b. Describe the setting that Jairus left in order to call out to the Lord. (Matthew 9:23-24) What tradition were his friends following? (Ruth 1:9; 1 Samuel 2:4)

c. Compare Jairus' attitude of hope for his daughter with the attitudes of others. (Matthew 9:18, 24; Mark 5:35, 38-40; Luke 8:49, 52-54)

179

d. In what ways might the story of Jairus and his daughter represent the spiritual authority of all fathers over their children? (Matthew 18:3; 19:14; 1 Peter 2:1, 2)

e. How did Jairus handle the crisis of his daughter's illness? (Matthew 9:18-25)

f. SUMMARY QUESTION: What lessons can be learned from Jairus about handling crises related to children? What are some other crises facing African American children today? How should they be handled?

5. Job and His Wife (Job 2:9, 10; 19:17; 31:10)

Job and his wife responded very differently to crisis.

a. What events let to Job's crisis? (Job 1:1, 13-21)

b. How did stress related to the crisis affect Job's body? (2:7)

c. Describe how Job's wife reacted to the crisis. (2:9) How did his friends respond? (2:11-13)

d. How did Job respond to the crisis? (1:22; 2:9-10)

e. How did Job's solution come? (Job 40--41; 42:12)

f. SUMMARY QUESTION: What principles can be learned from Job and his wife in crisis? In what ways are they similar to African Americans in crisis today?

6. FAMILY MINISTRY APPLICATION

What types of crises are facing African American families today? Using the contents of this chapter as a guide, draft a list of topics for a family ministry seminar focusing on handling crisis with faith.

7. PERSONAL APPLICATION

What is the most recent crisis that your family has faced? How did you handle it? What role did the Lord play? What did you learn?

CHAPTER TEN

Critical Issues Facing Black Families: SEXUALITY AND SUBSTANCE ABUSE

"Before healing others, heal thyself." (African Proverb)

Betty sat down at the table to tell Sam the news, while she took her daily vitamin supplements and her nightly smoke. Sam listened attentively while he opened his second can of beer. Betty told Sam that this morning, while she was taking her morning aspirins, she noticed a small bag of marijuana on the floor beside the toilet. It looked like it had fallen there by mistake.

Immediately she thought of her daughter Sandra. Sandra had been acting strangely lately. She would spend long hours away from home with her friends, but would never talk about where she had been or what she was doing with them.

"Have you noticed how she's been looking lately?" Sam asked Betty. "Her eyes look real glassy to me."

"She also seems kind of moody lately," Betty replied. "You know the police busted some of those kids over there at the high school last week. It was in all of the papers. Everyone was shocked to hear about a drug bust in Evanston."

"Yeah, Evanston has always been a quiet suburb," Sam said. "I guess the riffraff is getting out here."

181

By the time they finished talking, Betty had taken her usual sleeping pills and was ready for bed. Sam was pouring a "kicker" to go along with his third can of beer. Then they sat staring at the television screen, in silence.

As tragic as is the story of Sam and his family it is not nearly as tragic as that of John Everyday. John was a 17–year–old young man and rather athletic. He was the firstborn of three children. Having grown up in a family of three generations of a conservative Christian tradition, John was very religious and active in his large urban church. The church was started by his preacher grandfather who remained the senior pastor of the church. His father was one of the deacons and also the director of the church camp and Vacation Bible School.

I first met John in Bible study class. He impressed me as an articulate and quite knowledgeable young man who quoted the Bible rather extensively. I wondered if he really internalized any of what he was saying or if he was just repeating things he had heard all his life. He certainly said all the right things, I thought.

The second and the last time I saw John was in the emergency room when he was brought in by ambulance with chest pains. He was agitated, very warm to touch and his temperature registered 108 degrees. "My God," I said without thinking. What has gone wrong? John certainly could not have taken "crack," could he? Another young man, whose name I do not even recall, told me that John had been doing crack at school. Needless to say John died. His blood and urine tests confirmed that he took an overdose of cocaine in the form of "crack."

One of the biggest problems in the so–called "civilized" societies of the 20th century is excessive dependency on drugs. The drug orientation of the Western culture has reached such alarming proportions that the term "drug abuse" is not a term that is applied to excessive use of drugs but is limited to defining the illegal use of illegal drugs, only. That is, people are generally blind to drug abuse if it does not involve a drug listed as illegal.

However, in the above story, Betty, Sam and possibly their daughter Sandra, are all substance abusers. This chapter focuses on substance abuse. It explores the magnitude of the problem, and presents information which parents and people involved in family ministries need to know about various types of drugs and other substances. The chapter also provides guidelines for parents in detecting whether their child is a substance abuser, along with guidelines for steering children away from substance abuse. Also included is a core statement of a Christian perspective of sexuality which can be elaborated by the Christian education board.

The Magnitude of the Problem. In drug/substance abusing cultures, there is an enormous campaign by various advertising media, encouraging people to depend upon "legal" drugs. For example, when one cannot sleep at night one is no longer encouraged to drink hot cocoa, but to take the edge off with a sedative. When one gets tension headaches, one is no longer encouraged to relax through meditation, but to take an aspirin.

Today it is no longer enough to eat the right foods for our vitamin requirements. Instead we are asked to take ten, twenty, or even thirty vitamin tablets per day! Most people would not expect that vitamin pills are drugs, by any definition of the word. However this is just one example of the way our drug–oriented culture encourages abuse.

Commonly Abused Substances: Some of the most commonly abused substances are the hallucinogens or psychedelic drugs, known as "trippers" on the street. Opiated drugs or "hard drugs" are another category. Next there are the stimulants, or "uppers." Then there are the depressants or "downers," and there is alcohol.

"Trippers" (hallucinogens) cause users to hear and see things that are not really there. The things they hear and see are usually distorted and therefore frightening. Marijuana is in this category. Other terms for marijuana are "pot," "grass," and "weed."

Marijuana has been reported to have caused:
1) permanent brain damage
2) chromosomal damage and birth defects
3) chronic lung disease or bronchitis
4) sterility and impotence
5) lowered resistance to infection
6) lack of motivation

Following is a list of other drugs in the "tripper" category. Column #1 contains the name of the drug. Column #2 contains the names by which the drug is known on the street, and column #3 lists the complications the drug can cause.

DRUG	STREET NAME	COMPLICATIONS
Marijuana	grass, reefers, joint, pot, weed	poor judgment, genetic disorders
DOM	STP, peace, Tranquility	hallucinations, very poor judgment, distortions of reality
LSD and DMT	Acid, cubes	produces personality disorganization, "bad trips," panic, marked distortions of body image
Phencyclidine	PCP, angel dust	Marked, perpetual distortion and violent or aggressive behavior

"Hard drugs," or opiated drugs are somewhat stronger than "trippers." Heroin is the prototype of this group and is the most commonly used hard drug. When used either by injection or sniffing, it depresses the two vital functions of the body—the circulation system and the respiratory system. However, the ultimate complication from its use is death due to overdose. Other complications that heroin can cause are:
1) skin infections or boils
2) infection and damage of the heart valves
3) hepatitis
4) blood clots

Following is a list of drugs in the "hard drug" category.

Column #1 contains the name of the drug. Column #2 contains the names by which the drug is known on the street, and column #3 contains complications that can occur from its use.

DRUG	STREET NAME	COMPLICATIONS
Heroin	Horse, smack, junk	marked euphoria and other complications from overdose
Morphine	dollies	withdrawal can lead to death, stomach irritation, vomiting

"Uppers," or stimulants, are a category of drugs which includes amphetamines. These drugs elevate moods and energy levels. They also increase one's level of awareness and provide relief from fatigue. Amphetamines were once used as diet pills. Because of the properties of amphetamines, students often use them to prepare for examinations only to find themselves becoming addicted to them. The complications from uppers include:

1) skin, heart and liver infections, if the amphetamines are taken by injection

2) mental illness (psychosis) from long–term use

3) death due to overdose

Following is a list of drugs in the "upper" category. Column #1 contains the names of the drug. Column #2 contains the names by which the drug is known on the street, and column #3 contains complications that can occur from the use of it.

DRUG	STREET NAME	COMPLICATION
Amphetamine	Upper, peaches, hearts crystals, bennies, speed	agitation, heightened awareness aggressiveness, mental illness after prolonged use
Retalire	California sunshine	
Cocaine	coke, snow, crack	damage to the nose, such as perforation of septum. This is a clue to it use.

"Downers," or depressants, are another type of drug often abused in our society. These drugs depress the functions of the brain, heart, and breathing. They do everything that leads to death. Most sleeping pills fall into this category. Downers are the most dangerous drug of all. They kill from overdose and they kill from withdrawal. Because tolerance to these drugs develops, larger and larger doses are taken to produce the desired effect. This often leads to unintended overdoses.

Following is a list of drugs in the "downer" category. Column #1 contains the name of the drug. Column #2 contains the name by which the drug is known on the street, and column #3 contains complications that can occur from the use of it.

DRUG	STREET NAME	COMPLICATIONS
Nembutal	Barks	depresses circulation
Seconal	Downers	depresses breathing and brain function
Amytal	Red Devils	extremely addictive
Tuinal	blue devils, rainbows, blue birds, double trouble	death from overdose or withdrawal

Long before one feels the "high" of alcohol many of the person's functions are already significantly depressed. Most important of these are his/her reflexes. In fact one does not have to feel drunk in order to become dangerous on the highway. One feels "high" on alcohol initially only because those areas of the brain that inhibit or control wild and erratic behavior are first depressed. With the control of wild behavior thus depressed one feels more liberated, giving the false sense of a "high."

Alcohol has to be recognized as a drug. Like most drugs it has bad and serious side effects. It is also extremely addicting. Not only is it addicting, but the body quickly develops tolerance to it. One has to drink more and more alcohol as time goes on, in order to get the same "high." But the body's ability to detoxify alcohol is limited. Regardless of how much alcohol is ingested the body can only detoxify limited amounts. For an average man of 150 lbs. the amount is 0.034 ounces per hour. This translates to only 3/10th of an ounce every hour. So, the rest of the alcohol stays in the body and the body is exposed to its harmful effects until it is detoxified. The direct effect of alcohol is considerable and can lead to death.

Detecting Substance Abuse in Children. It is a mistake to assume that children are Christians and therefore not susceptible to drug abuse. Christian children are subjected to the same forces that pressure other children. Parents must actively guide them in order for them to resist these pressures. God will protect the children. However, parents and relatives must be instruments which God uses to protect the children.

Drug abuse in children begins in various ways, the three most common of which are:

1) propaganda from advertising media
2) peer group pressure
3) insufficient inner strength
4) insufficient external support from parents and from the church

While open communication is one sure way of detecting and preventing a child from experimenting with drugs, it is difficult to detect whether a child is experimenting with drugs until s/he has used them often enough to become addicted, particularly with the newer forms of cocaine which take only a few tries to become addicted. However, a few classic signs can help parents become concerned about their children:

1) a change in the child's behavior
2) "glassy eyes"
3) unwillingness of the child to discuss the time spent with friends

What can a parent do? There is very little any one person or group can do about the culture. Pressure from the culture will continue to be exerted on America's children. What we can do, however, is prepare our children to survive in the culture. The reality is that we can only partially protect our children.

No parents, very attentive or not, can be with their children all the time. In a culture which is so pervaded with the idea of using drugs for everything it is practically impossible to protect the children all the time. Parents definitely cannot do it alone. However, we can provide the children with the tools they can use to protect themselves.

Firstly parents together with the church can lead the children to develop inner strength which comes from being one with God. Being one with God!! That means the child's entire existence is with God. While eating he/she is doing it with God. While learning in school he/she is doing it with God. While going to movies he/she is doing it with God. With such oneness with God the child has the inner strength on which he/she can rely.

Secondly parents can teach the children about drug abuse. To do this parents must learn about drug abuse. Actually parents do find out in the process of learning about drug abuse that they themselves are too drug centered. That is the first step in training their children to be drug free.

Developing a Christian View of Human Sexuality. This very important part of our life has been largely neglected by the Christian church, even though the Scriptures give clear principles about this area of our development. In some communities there has been a battleground of controversy between home and school on the issue of sex education. Responsibility for instruction should rest with the home but given the overwhelming demands placed upon the family, this important task should be shared among home, school and church. Understanding one's sexuality involves so much more than just the imparting of information about sex. It includes taking on gender identity, learning sex roles descriptions, understanding sexual behavior, acquiring the knowledge and dispositions that allow a person to develop intimate, loving relationships and function sexually. Every aspect, practically, is laden with values and beliefs.

Disciples of Jesus Christ should impart Christian values about this central part of life which can be a source of great satisfaction, great frustration or great problems. The sexual permissiveness which pervades our world, the breakdown of family life and the wide range of individual circumstances have often led to insensitivity about approaching these issues.

Ideally the Christian Education Board in every church should offer training for parents on:

1. How to rear children with clear–cut gender identity.
2. Parenting skills on transmitting masculine and feminine roles (what does it mean to be a Black man or woman).
3. How to teach children about sex which should include not only the facts of conception and birth but sexually transmitted diseases as well.
4. How to inculcate psychologically sound and biblically based values about relationships, love, and marriage. Not only must they have these values but they should be able to articulate them in their language to their peers.
5. The importance of providing well–balanced, supervised activities (lots of them) for young people. Through role–playing and drama, teach them how to plan dates, carry on meaningful conversations and defuse potentially sexually intimate situations until the proper time.

In addition the church should provide instruction and support for its members of all ages in human sexuality. Principles such as the following should be emphasized:

1. It is Christian for women and men to accept their bodies as good, a creation of God. It is normal for them to become educated concerning the nature, purpose and functions of their bodies. There are those who believe that to be close to God and truly spiritual is to deny one's sexuality. However, biblical writings are remarkably candid about sexual matters. The very highest and holiest relationship between God and man and woman is likened to the intimacy of the honeymoon of the bride and groom.

2. Poor sexual attitudes are learned early in life. Sexual abuse,

fear, worry, anger, guilt and resentment can completely block out loving feelings and separate physical desire from tenderness, protection and commitment.

3. God has given us our minds and our will in order to control our emotions. We are responsible both male and female for our behavior. Powerful as the sex drive may be at certain periods in our life, it is a drive that can be released appropriately in heterosexual marriage or redirected in other wholesome activity. Chastity is never easy but God does give grace for this struggle.

4. The Bible condemns sexual behavior related to the dishonesty of adultery, the violence resulting from coveting another's spouse, and unnatural sex of incest and homosexuality. Jesus added the deeper admonition against lusting (Matthew 5:27-28) which can be defined as the pursuit of physical desire without love or commitment.

5. There are major differences between physical attraction and love. Adequate information about physical, emotional, intellectual, and sexual responsibility should be given before and during marriage as well as for singles, divorcees, widows, and widowers.

6. People of all ages need to know how to positively develop loving relationships and how to minimize the temptations of unhealthy attitudes, un–Christian values, and irresponsible behavior which often originate in the workplace and the social arena. With the decreasing pool of eligible Black males, a major effort needs to be launched by the church to reclaim and reeducate Black males for responsible behavior in this area.

Summary. Abuses of God given sexuality, like additions are a usurpation of God's authority and order. As such they displace God plan for an individual's preference. Therefore, they are selfish in nature and eventually lead to moral decline. Families need to be given accurate information, biblical principles and support in applying them in the complicated situations of contemporary society.

BIBLE FAMILIES

INSTRUCTIONS: The following exercises allow you to apply principles from this chapter to the analysis of biblical families who had members who were substance abusers or involved in sexual relationships. The first five exercises consist of five "fill–in–the–blank" discovery questions and a summary question. The sixth exercise allows you to apply the principles to a church–based family ministry. The seventh exercise allows for personal application.

Noah

"And Noah began to be an husbandman, and he planted a vineyard: And he drank of the wine, and was drunken; and he was uncovered within his tent. And Ham, the father of Canaan, saw the nakedness of his father, and told his two brethren without. And he said, cursed be Canaan; a servant of servants shall he be unto his brethren." (Genesis 9:20-22, 25)

Lot

"And Lot went up out of Zoar, and dwelt in the mountain, and his two daughters with him...And they made their father drink wine that night: and the firstborn went in, and lay with her father...and the younger arose, and lay with him; and he perceived not when she lay down, nor when she arose. Thus were both the daughters of Lot with child by their father." (Genesis 19:30, 33, 35-36)

Adam and Eve

"And the Lord God commanded the man, saying, Of every tree of the garden thou mayest freely eat: But of the tree of the knowledge of good and evil, thou shalt not eat of it: for in the day that thou eatest thereof thou shalt surely die. And when the woman saw that the tree was good for food...she took of the fruit thereof, and did eat, and gave also unto her husband with her; and he did eat...and Adam and his wife hid themselves from the presence of the Lord God..." (Genesis 2:16–17; 3:6, 8)

Ahasuerus and Vashti

"And when these days were expired, the king made a feast unto all the people...And they gave them drink in vessels of gold...and royal wine in abundance...On the seventh day, when the heart of the king was merry with wine, he commanded...To bring Vashti the queen before the king with the crown royal, to show the people and the princes her beauty...But the queen Vashti refused to come at the king's commandment...therefore was the king very wroth, and his anger burned in him." (Esther 1:5, 7, 10-12)

Ben–hadad

"And it came to pass, when Ben-hadad heard this message, as he was drinking, he and the kings in the pavilions, that he said unto his servants, Set yourselves in array...And they went out at noon. But Ben-hadad was

drinking himself drunk in the pavilions, he and the kings...And the young men of the princes of the provinces went out first; and Ben-hadad sent out...So these young men of the princes of the provinces came out of the city...And they slew every one his man: and the Syrians fled; and Israel pursued them: and Ben-haded the king of Syria escaped on an horse with the horsemen." (1 Kings 20:12, 16-17, 19-20)

1. Lot: Substance Abuse and Incest (Genesis 19:30-38)

Incest is not new. It dates back at least as far as Lot. It is usually connected, in some way, with substance abuse.

a. Describe the instability in Lot's childhood and early adulthood. (Genesis 11:28, 31-32; 12:1-4, 10; 13:1, 5-12; 14:11-12, 15-16) How might this have "driven Lot to drink"?

b. How did Lot come to live in a cave (19:1-30), with his family? How might this have "driven Lot to drink"?

c. How did his daughter respond to the uncertainty and instability in their lives? (19:30-38)

d. What was one result of Lot's daughter's sins? (Deuteronomy 2:9-11; 23:3-4; Genesis 14:5; Ruth 1:1, 2; Numbers 22:1; 25:1-2; Isaiah 16:14)

e. What was another result of Lot's daughter's sins? (Deuteronomy 23:3, 4; 1 Kings 11:7; Judges 3:13; 2 Samuel 10:1-19; Psalm 83:5-137; Nehemiah 4:1-3)

f. SUMMARY QUESTION: Are there any similarities between the circumstances surrounding the incest in Lot's family and incest in families today? What is the probable role of substance abuse?

2. Ben-Hadad I (1 Kings 20:1-11)

Substance abuse played a major role in Ben-Hadad's life.

a. Who was Ben-Hadad? In what family was he? (1 Kings 15:18; 2 Chronicles 16:1-4; 1 Kings 11:23)

b. What type personality did Ben-Hadad have? (20:1-11)

c. What role did substance abuse play in Ben-Hadad's life? (20:12, 18) How did if affect his actions?

d. What was the eventual outcome of Ben-Hadad's drinking? (20:19-30)

e. In what ways might alcoholism have caused Ben-Hadad to die of a disease, rather than old age? (2 Kings 8:7-15)

f. SUMMARY QUESTION: What impact did substance abuse have on the royal family of Ben-Hadad? What effect is substance abuse having on African American families today?

3. Ahasuerus and Vashti (Esther 1:5-22)

Substance abuse can wreck a marriage.

a. Who were Ahasuerus and Vashti? (Esther 1:1-3, 9) What was their life–style? (1:3-9)

b. How much drinking went on at their parties? (1:7-8, 10)

c. In what ways did alcohol affect Ahasuerus' personality? (1:3-11)

d. In your opinion, why might Vashti have refused to parade before Ahasuerus' guests? (1:3-12)

e. What effect did alcohol have on the marriage of Vashti and Ahasuerus? (1:10-22; 2:1-2)

f. SUMMARY QUESTION: What lessons can be learned from the marriage of Vashti and Ahasuerus? Are there any modern parallels?

4. Adam and Eve (Genesis 1:15—3:8)

We abuse substances when we use them in ways that God did not intend.

a. Who were Adam and Eve? (Genesis 1:27-31; 2:7, 18, 21-25; 3:20)

b. Describe the setting in which Adam and Eve lived. (2:1-17)

c. What restrictions were placed on the tree of knowledge? (2:16-17)

d. How did it happen that Adam and Eve abused the substance of the tree of knowledge? (3:1-6)

e. What effect did their substance abuse have on themselves and future generations? (3:7-24; 4:1-11)

f. SUMMARY QUESTION: What lessons can be learned from the marriage of Adam and Eve?

5. Noah and the Fruit of the Vine (Genesis 9:18-29)

Substance abuse was a problem for Noah.

a. Who were Noah and his children? (Genesis 6:5-9)

b. In what type environment were Noah's children raised? (6:5-12) How might this have affected their sense of morality?

c. How did Noah and his family survive the flood? (6:12-22)

d. What effect did substance abuse have, first on Noah and then on his family? (9:18-24)

e. Which son of Ham was cursed as a result of this incident? (10:6; 9:25-27)

f. SUMMARY QUESTION: What can be learned from the family of Noah about alcoholism?

6. FAMILY MINISTRY APPLICATION

Based on this chapter and the study of substance abusing families in the Bible, develop a list of topics for a seminar on substance abuse, its effects on sexuality, and today's African American families.

7. PERSONAL APPLICATION

What role does substance abuse play in your extended family? Has the drug culture made an impact? Is there a relationship between it and sexuality? What steps can you take to solve the problem?

CHAPTER ELEVEN

EDUCATING FOR SURVIVAL

**"Being prepared beforehand is better than afterthought."
(African Proverb)**

Cassandra sat at the end of the long table, watching as the other "Ebony Entrepreneurs" entered. The Ebony Entrepreneurs is one of the ministries of Holy Cross Church. It brings together women from the church and the surrounding community and teaches them how to form and operate their own businesses.

Cassandra remembered how, at first, she didn't want to be bothered with any church women. From as far back as she could remember, all the church women she knew ever did was criticize her and tattle about her to her mother. However, today, with two children, a third child on the way, no husband and no job, Cassandra had not been in a position to refuse help when these particular church women stopped by her home one day.

She remembered how, after she was in the program for a while, she got a sense that the women from this church really cared about her and the other women from her neighborhood. That is one reason that, once she got in the training program, she also decided to accept Christ as her personal Saviour and join the church. As she sat there waiting for the session to begin and watching the women take their places around the table, she was really thankful.

> *Her neighbor Sally now owned a catering service.*
> *Her cousin Nancy ran a day care center out of her*
> *home, and Jennifer, Cassandra's best friend since*
> *childhood, now had a "meals on wheels" company*
> *that catered to senior citizens. Cassandra herself ran*
> *a telephone answering service and a light secretarial*
> *service from her home. None of the women were on*
> *welfare anymore. All of them were saved, and their*
> *children were now in Sunday School. "It seems like*
> *there's a sense of peace in the air these days," Cas-*
> *sandra thought, smiling.*

The program at Holy Cross Church represents a new trend in Christian ministry. Programs such as the Ebony Entrepreneurs at Holy Cross, represent a broadened concept of family ministry, Christian Education, and evangelism. Churches such as Holy Cross have discovered that ministries to modern African American families must be flexible, creative, and willing to become involved with all areas of family life, which until recently some churches hesitated to enter.

This chapter focuses on the need to equip heads of African American households through training and education. It discusses how churches can approach this, and why training should be considered a ministry of the church. Creative approaches to developing such ministries are presented, along with some ways that churches can put families into touch with community training resources.

The Need. We have reached a point, in America, where a high percentage of African American families are no longer able to function as families are supposed to function. Many low–income Black families and quite a few other families can no longer carry out traditional family functions. Black men are unemployed or underemployed in exceptionally high numbers, as are Black teenagers. Many Black men are imprisoned and are not receiving an education or relevant job training. Most juvenile offenders and prisoners are high school drop–outs. Men and women who for years have held steady employment are finding the need for retraining in a new career as industries and companies fail or merge. More women are required to work for longer periods in order to enable the family to remain economically independent.

A large percentage of African American families are single parent families, headed by women. Often these single women are quite young. They do not have financial resources, largely because they do not have adequate educational skills. Neither do they have money for adequate child care. This problem itself cuts off their educational opportunities. While some of them will return to junior high school or high school, few will go beyond high school. Even if they ever complete high school, once they have a baby most do not have marketable skills.

However, we now live in a world where a high school education is not sufficient for earning a living or for maintaining oneself or one's children. Therefore one of the major needs for African American families is education and training.

This may sound like quite a hopeless situation. Despite its criticalness, there is hope. The hope resides in the spiritual resources God's people have available in responding to these needs. Romans 12:1, 2 makes reference to the transforming or renewing of our minds. This is a necessity if we are to meet these massive needs head on. It involves adopting God's mindset which Jesus Christ demonstrated in His holistic approach to humankind. He wept for all His people but followed a well thought out plan so His efforts produced possibilities for re–creation for those who chose to avail themselves. People were fed and sheltered, bodies were healed, minds were taught, lessons were demonstrated, emotions were accepted but put in balance in Jesus' ministry.

God's people must begin to think and then act like their God. Rather than being repelled, overwhelmed or detached from the needy let us view them through renewed minds that respond with love/action in offering services aimed at the root causes of hopelessness and poverty.

Practically, the implications of such a mindset would lead a congregation to consider its fundamental needs and those of their outreach community for education in all aspects of life, such as:

a. Biblical values and teaching

b. Supplemental academic preparation

c. World history with a focus on the contributions and culture of Africa and African Americans

d. Critical thinking

e. Career guidance and training

f. Marriage preparation and enrichment

g. Parenting skills

h. Health and medical practices

i. Consumer and legal issues

j. Job search skills and job bank information

k. Literacy training for the poor and nonreaders

The education sponsored by the church will differ from that offered by other institutions in that it is centered in a godly world view, integrated with other truth and delivered by caring competent persons who believe in the abilities of its students, hold them accountable and provide structure and discipline along the way. This holistic approach to education and training offers spiritual values, motivation, and psychological support as it imparts practical knowledge.

Black people love words and language and are attracted to careers requiring the oral tradition. Our forefathers were also the founders of philosophy, science, and mathematics. They were theorists and technicians. More African Americans need to know this and imitate the teaching methods of the ancients who produced students committed to nothing less than excellence. Our young people require career guidance in order to explore career paths for the new workplace. Careers in the allied health field, paralegal, computer repair, telecommunications, information processing are only a few.

There is a need for programs which equip young people and single parents, in particular, to use their natural gifts and curiosity in the high tech world in which we now live. To survive in this economy, they will need well developed communications skills, along with marketable skills needed by the contemporary workplace.

How the Church Can Become Involved. Today the Black church needs to become the lost extended family which is no longer functional for so many people. In order to minister to families effectively, the church needs to assume responsibility for some of the functions that were once those of the extended family. In addition to this, the church needs to equip each member of the family system.

One way to approach this is to create innovative, church–based ministries. This might involve writing grant proposals to get money from foundations and government agencies. Another approach would be for the church to refer people to resources available in the community for training and education, while providing support services which enable people to complete their programs. These include providing transportation, books, child care and tuition loans.

Ministering to young children and their parents in this way is one of the first things a Board of Christian Education might want to place on its agenda.

Ministering through Literacy Training. A major barrier to employment is illiteracy. Many young single parents and older adults are illiterate, and many cannot even complete a job application. Another arm of the church's ministry can provide literacy training to illiterate members.

Money from foundations, government agencies and schools is available for this purpose. Community colleges have some of this money, and will fund and offer organizational assistance to local churches who wish to sponsor such programs within their facilities. Money from city, local, state, federal, and even some county agencies is also available.

However, convincing a person to reenter training and school after the traumatic experience of having a family involves more than just telling them where they can locate literacy training. It involves working with them psychologically. The person will need to be motivated and teamed up with a mentor friend.

Ministering by Equipping Grandmothers and Grandfathers. If the church is to relate to every member of the extended family, it cannot ignore the grandmothers and grandfathers. For it is the grandmother in many families who bears the responsibility for raising the grandchildren. Grandmothers also need to be taught to prepare children for today's world, for today's world is very different from the world in which they were raised.

Some universities and churches have opened day care centers where grandmothers come with their grandchildren and watch while the children are taught language, reading and critical thinking skills. At these centers, the grandparents are taught parenting for today's world. They soon realize that their home is not merely a place where the chores of raising a new generation of children take place. The centers become places where grandmothers have social contact and group support while completing classes.

Ministering Through Day Care. As mentioned before, there is a tremendous need for day care, so that mothers can return to school and can work. One way of ministering to single parents would be for churches to offer free or subsidized child care. Child care is such a big expense for so many single parents and rarely offers moral training. Rarely is it available during the weekends and evenings when many parents must work or want to attend classes. We prefer to offer subsidized care because we like parents to pay a little money, if possible. In this way, they have an investment in the place. Those who can't pay can offer service. It is possible to offer this for mothers with children from six weeks of age, through school age. It is reasonable to require parents who receive these services to attend parenting classes once or twice a month.

Ministering by Developing Apartment Complexes for Single and Low–Income Parents. In addition to not being able to locate suitable child care, many low–income single parents also have trouble locating suitable housing. These are two of the most significant barriers to becoming a part of the mainstream of society. However, churches can relate to both of these needs while at the same time equipping the children involved for their future role in the world and in the church.

Churches can develop apartment complexes for single parents in the same way that they develop such places for senior citizens. However, built into these apartments for single parents could be Christian Day Schools. At these schools, Christian Education for children would be taught. The church could use its vans to pick up the children and take them to the centers. These could be the same vans that pick them up for Sunday School, etc. In fact, the center could offer classes at times when their mothers are at choir rehearsal, training hour, and weekday Bible study.

Staffing at the center could be done by having the mothers work cooperatively. In fact, day care centers could be places where mothers also acquire some job–related skills, such as answering telephones, learning computer skills, doing light clerical work, and serving as teacher aides.

At these centers, Christian Education classes for the children would be offered. Consequently, the church becomes an active participant in interrupting the cycle of poverty in which so many mothers and grandmothers have been trapped.

The centers could also be places where single parents engage in cooperative purchasing of food, clothing, etc., and save money.

Ministering by Acquiring Federal Funds. A number of federally funded programs are available to community institutions for training single parents and others. For example, the Job Training Partnership Act (JTPA), through which federal money is allocated to every state, is for free training programs for single parents. Another is the Carl Perkins Act. Through this act, money is given to every state to provide training for single parents and displaced homemakers (women who have been out of the work force for more than five years and need to upgrade their employment skills). One center received a quarter of a million dollars through this act alone to train single parents and displaced homemakers. This center provides free child care, payment for books, free training, and money for transportation.

Through this program, 25 single parents were placed in an automated office skills training program. The center will help place them when they complete the program. Some funds are still available. There is a need for someone on the Board of Christian Education to apply for, collect, and direct the resources into various areas of our churches where people in the church and community can access it for training.

Financial aid for attending community colleges and universities is also available. It is true that financial aid was reduced during the Reagan administration. However, there is still a considerable amount of money available from a variety of sources. We must be willing to persist in locating it. The colleges themselves have information. However, other resources exist. Individuals need to apply at least 8 to 12 weeks prior to the time they wish to enter school.

Thousands of single parents are working and attending school while raising their children. Completing school in these circumstances may require more time than it ordinarily would, but that doesn't matter. What matters is that the single parent now has a goal, and is working toward something that s/he feels s/he can achieve. This is a major accomplishment in itself.

Ministering by Teaching Entrepreneurial Skills. So many single parents are very creative and talented. With a little skill, they could be taught to run their own businesses. We have witnessed many of them do so well as entrepreneurs. Many do exceptionally well with budgeting if they begin with home–based businesses, are prepared for hard work and are offering needed services or products. Many have had to manage on such small amounts of money that they have already acquired some of the skills they need.

More mature, displaced homemakers also have business skills. They have raised families, coordinated programs, served in the churches and done volunteer work. With some training, they could now be able to enter the job market realistically and can become independent heads of homes.

Owning one's own business is another way to bypass some racial, gender and age discrimination. Because single parents are hard workers, owning their own businesses would be an ideal way to achieve a certain amount of independence from some of the negative realities of living in a low–income, unsafe neighborhood. A home–based business is an ideal place to start since it is very difficult to obtain loans these days.

Entrepreneurship involves risk taking. Statistics reflect that most new businesses do not survive beyond the first few years. However, statistics also reflect that females have started businesses about five to one for every male that has done so in the last five years. Statistics also indicate that women are far more successful than men who start businesses, particularly if they begin their businesses within the home and cooperate with several others.

An example is a woman who came through one such program in Texas. She started a shoe shine business with $50.00. You know what she did? She went to a large commercial building (like Merchandise Mart in Chicago), and asked them for free space because it was a service that would contribute to their complex. With the $50.00, she had someone make one of those wooden boxes and purchased her supplies. Then she started shining shoes. Now that lady has 10 of these places in the largest office buildings in Dallas. She has hired people. Now she goes from one site to the other, collecting, supervising and managing.

Another woman started a home–based business in her garage. Others have started them in apartments. One woman started hers in a one–bedroom apartment. She does secretarial work, typing and editing. She finally got to the point where she could purchase an inexpensive word processor. Now she offers word processing services for businesses which can't afford to hire a secretary. These businesses lease out their clerical work to her.

Still another woman started an answering service out of her home. In this way she could be with her children, while earning money. She avoided all of the expenses that are a part of going out to work. These are expenses which can use up all of one's money.

Then there are those who become partners. Two women formed a team. One did the bookkeeping and the other did the sales. Together they operated a catering business. It wasn't just the usual catering business. They specialized in weddings. They have done a wonderful job.

These success stories should inspire new job training ministries in churches throughout the country. The church can teach people, encourage good business practices and support church members' businesses as was true earlier in our history.

Summary. This chapter has focused on the need to equip Black families with education and training. It has discussed innovative ways in which the African American church can minister to people who need education and training in order to locate employment. These innovations include: teaching sex education, providing literacy training, equipping grandmothers, providing day care, developing apartment complexes for single parents, acquiring federal funds to support training programs, and teaching entrepreneurship.

The following exercise provides the opportunity for applying some of the information presented in this chapter to the analysis of a biblical family.

BIBLE FAMILIES

INSTRUCTIONS: The exercises which follow provide the opportunity to study several highly trained people from the Bible, their impact on the Community of Faith, and the role their families played in their development. The first five exercises consist of "fill–in–the–blank" discovery questions and a summary question. The sixth exercise allows you to apply the knowledge gained to a church–based family ministry. The seventh question allows for personal application.

Apollos

"And a certain Jew named Apollos, born at Alexandria, an eloquent man, and mighty in the scriptures, came to Ephesus. And he began to speak boldly in the synagogue: whom when Aquila and Priscilla had heard, they took him unto them, and expounded unto him the way of God more perfectly. And when he was disposed to pass into Achaia, the brethren wrote, exhorting the disciples to receive him: who, when he was come, helped them much which had believed through grace: For he mightily convinced the Jews, and that publicly, showing by the scriptures that Jesus was Christ." (Acts 18:24, 26–28)

The Ethiopian Eunuch

"And he arose and went: and, behold, a man of Ethiopia, an eunuch of great authority under Candace queen of the Ethiopians, who had the charge of all her treasure, and had come to Jerusalem for to worship, Was returning, and sitting in his chariot read Esaias the prophet. Then the Spirit said unto Philip, Go near, and join thyself to this chariot. And as they went on their way, they came unto a certain water: and the eunuch said, See, here is water; what doth hinder me to be baptized? And he commanded the chariot to stand still: and they went down both into the water, both Philip and the eunuch; and he baptized him." (Acts 8:27–29, 36, 38)

Huldah

"So Hilkiah the priest, and Ahikam, and Achbor, and Shaphan, and Asahiah, went unto Huldah the prophetess, the wife of Shallum the son of Tikvah, the son of Harhas, keeper of the wardrobe; (now she dwelt in Jerusalem in the college;) and they communed with her. And she said unto them, Thus saith the Lord God of Israel, Tell the man that sent you to me." (2 Kings 2:14–15)

Ezra

"This Erza went up from Babylon; and he was a ready scribe in the law of Moses, which the Lord God of Israel had given: and the king granted him all his

request, according to the hand of the Lord his God upon him." (Erza 7:6)

Bezaleel

"See, I have called by name Bezaleel the son of Uri, the son of Hur, of the tribe of Judah: And I have filled him with the spirit of God, in wisdom, and in understanding, and in knowledge, and in all manner of workmanship, And I, behold, I have given with him Aholiab, the son of Ahisamach, of the tribe of Dan: and in the hearts of all that are wisehearted I have put wisdom, that they may make all that I commanded thee." (Exodus 31:2–3, 6)

1. Bezaleel (Exodus 31:2–11)

The Lord used Bezaleel's knowledge in the building of His tabernacle.

a. To what family did Bezaleel belong? (Exodus 31:2; 1 Chronicles 2:19, 20)

b. What famous towns did Bezaleel's relatives found? (1 Chronicles 2:50–51)

c. Of what importance was Bethlehem, one of the towns Bezaleel's relatives founded? (1 Chronicles 2:31; Micah 5:2; Ruth 1:1, 2; 2:1, 4, 11; 1 Samuel 16:1; 2 Samuel 23:15; Matthew 2:1)

d. What gifts did the Lord give Bezaleel? (Exodus 31:3–6)

e. How did the Lord use Bezaleel's knowledge? (31:6–11)

f. SUMMARY QUESTION: What was the likely role of Bezaleel's family and the Community of Faith in honing his skills for service? What lessons can be learned from this family?

2. Huldah (2 Kings 22:14–20)

The Lord used Huldah's knowledge of prophecy to help others understand a newly found Book of the Law.

a. Who was Shallum, Huldah's husband? (2 Kings 22:14; 2 Chronicles 34:20–22; Jeremiah 32:6–7)

b. Who was Huldah's extended family? (2 Kings 22:14)

c. What role did Huldah play in the Community of Faith? (2 Kings 22:14–20)

d. What role did a prophetess play in Israel? (Deuteronomy 13:1; 18:9, 15, 20)

e. How did Huldah likely become prepared for her role in Israel? (2 Kings 2:1–5)

f. SUMMARY QUESTION: What was the likely role of Huldah's family and the Community of Faith in honing Huldah's gifts for service? What lessons can today's families learn from Huldah's family?

3. Ezra (Ezra 7)

The Lord used Ezra's talents to create permanent records of His interactions with humankind.

a. To what family did Ezra belong? (Ezra 7:1–5)

b. Describe his extended family. (Nehemiah 11:17; 2 Kings 22:8; 23:2)

c. What was Ezra's role in the Community of Faith? (Ezra 7:11–28)

d. How did Ezra become prepared for his job? (7:6, 9–10, 27, 28; 8:22, 31)

e. Did knowledge cause Ezra to forget about God? Explain. (9:1–15)

f. SUMMARY QUESTION: What was the likely role of Ezra's family and the Community of Faith in honing his skills for service? What lessons can modern families learn from Ezra's family?

4. Apollos (Acts 18:24–28)

The Lord used Apollos' gifts in the Community of Faith.

a. Where was Apollos' original family? (Alexandria is in Egypt on the continent of Africa.) What does this tell us about the likely race of Apollos? (Acts 18:24)

b. What other information does the Bible provide about Apollos' hometown? (Acts 2:1–5, 10; 6:8–12; 27:6)

c. What role did Apollos eventually play in the Community of Faith? (18:27, 27; 19:1; 1 Corinthians 3:4–7; Titus 3:13)

d. How did Apollos prepare for his role in the Community of Faith? (Acts 18:24–26)

e. Who was Apollos' surrogate Christian family? (18:24–26; Titus 3:13)

f. SUMMARY QUESTION: What was the likely role of Apollos' family and that of the Community of Faith in his personal development? What lessons can modern families and churches learn from Apollos' life?

5. The Ethiopian Eunuch (Acts 8:27–38)

The Ethiopian Eunuch probably caused the spread of the Gospel in Ethiopia. He was a scholar and a highly skilled man.

a. Ethiopia is an African country. What are some of the images of Ethiopia that occur in Scripture? (2 Chronicles 14:9; Jeremiah 13:23)

b. What are some prophecies concerning Ethiopia in Scripture? (Isaiah 18:1–7; 45:11–17; Zephaniah 3:8–12)

c. Who was the Ethiopian Eunuch and what was his role in Ethiopia? (Isaiah 56:1–8; Matthew 19:11–12; Acts 8:27)

d. What evidence is there that the Ethiopian Eunuch was a scholar? (8:27, 30–34)

e. What did the Ethiopian Eunuch learn from the passage he was reading and how did this affect his life? (8:32–39)

f. SUMMARY QUESTION: The Ethiopian Eunuch's family is not mentioned in Scripture. It is quite possible that he was single. If you had been Philip, how might you have explained to him how Jesus can meet his need for family? (8:32–33; Isaiah 56:1–7) What implications does his story have for ministry to modern singles?

6. FAMILY MINISTRY APPLICATION

What are some ways in which the local church can put African American families in touch with educational and training opportunities? Can the local church itself offer training opportunities? If so, how?

7. PERSONAL APPLICATION

Are there ways in which you can enhance the performance of your ministry with training? If so, how? What action will you take?

CHAPTER TWELVE

AFRICAN AMERICAN FAMILY MINISTRY

"The man who has bread to eat does not appreciate the severity of a famine." (African Proverb)

It had been about a year since the Chrysler plant had closed, leaving a majority of the residents in the community surrounding Beacon Street Baptist Church unemployed. Since this happened, there had been a rise in various social problems throughout the area. A number of people from the community surrounding the church had approached various church members for help. There was also an increase in the number of requests by members of Beacon Street Church for counseling.

Several homeless families sought counseling through the church's soup kitchen where they came for meals. A number of female members of the church had reported to various deacons that their husbands had recently become violent and abusive to their children. The Youth Director reported that a number of teenagers came to him asking for help because their parents were spending their money on alcohol and cocaine and didn't have enough money to provide them with meals.

The deacons reported a number of seniors who were forced to retire before they had planned. Others had lost businesses which were affected by the plant clos-

213

ing. Consequently there was a rise in depressed senior citizen members of the church. Another disturbing trend was an increase in reported rapes, some of the victims being teenagers from the church. The mothers of these teenagers and their daughters had become depressed and asked for counseling.

Nearly every church leader had been approached by such depressed people. In fact, the ministerial staff had received so many requests for help that the ministers could not handle all of them. The church therefore decided to install a counseling ministry, and to train lay counselors to assist depressed people who reached out to the church for help.

Every person mentioned in the above story is a member of a family. Each family represented in this story is obviously undergoing stress of one type or another. This is true of the lay counselors at the church and of the people they are attempting to serve. While the particular situation described may seem extreme, some variation of it exists in African American communities throughout the United States.

As economic and related psychological realities continue to inflict pain in the African American community, afflicted families will continue to reach out to the African American church for help. This chapter is designed to help those who attempt to serve hurting families, through local church ministries. It focuses on some of the problems that African American families are encountering, and it provides guidelines for helping lay counselors in local churches to minister to such persons.

What is family ministry? Any serious consideration of church ministry to the African American family must be preceded by an understanding of four basic issues that critically affect Black families:

1. The roles we want African American children to play in our community in particular and in the society in general when they become adults.
2. The training of our children which was traditionally done by the family and which is now progressively declining.
3. The miseducation or lack of education of African American children in the nation's school systems. (Read Carter Woodson's book, *The Miseducation of the Negro*.)
4. The general breakdown of the African American nuclear and extended family.

First, rearing children is primarily bringing up and preparing them for the roles they are expected to assume. Traditionally the family is the institution of such early training; the school takes over later. Society at large determines which roles the children are expected to play when they become adults. Society therefore develops institutions and controls our communities to ensure that most of the children are trained for their projected roles.

When the society at large defines goals and roles for a particular subgroup of the society which are destructive or demeaning to that subgroup, it is incumbent on that subgroup to define its own goals and roles. It is not simple for a subgroup to always define its own roles. The methods used by the larger society to enforce the roles of any subgroup are often subtle and at times violent. As such it has been the goal of some part of American society to have African Americans perform primarily manual labor and the children were so trained by various means. Now that the economic base has changed, the society's goal and role for African Americans has also changed. A large proportion of African Americans and Hispanic populations are not expected to play any meaningful role in society. Some have estimated that up to 50% of African American men are expected to play no meaningful role in society. We have been trained from childhood to accept this role and many of our communities in fact have accepted it, or we feel helpless to change the condition. To survive this oppressive expectation the African American community has to define its own goals and roles. It is absolutely mandatory for African Americans to define the roles we prepare to play and train our children accordingly.

Second, early childhood training has been traditionally the responsibility of the family. In the African American community both the nuclear family (mother, father, and children) and the extended family are breaking down rapidly.

If the family is disintegrating, then our children are not getting the training they need in most cases. The implication is unmistakable. Someone else is defining our goals and roles for us, and training our children to play those roles. We believe that someone should step in and do what the family has failed to do. The church, we feel, is the logical institution to fulfill this mission.

Third, the education of our children should accomplish two general objectives. It should lead them to understand everything they could possibly understand about the larger society, and it should lead them to understand thoroughly their heritage, their past. Anything less than this is a miseducation of our children. If the schools cannot or do not want to accomplish these two objectives then we must find ways of doing it in the church.

Fourth, the disintegration of the family must be reversed. We believe that the church must play an active role in strengthening the family. For the church must clearly understand what is happening to African Americans in particular and men of color in general. The church must acknowledge what it believes in. It must understand how a person or a group of persons can say they believe in God, or they are Christians and at the same time treat African Americans and other non–white groups as inferior people.

Consider the case of Jeff. Jeff is a 10–year–old African American boy who dreams of becoming a scientist. On Friday during his science class his teacher made a statement which this 10–year–old boy knew to be false. The boy correctly stated that the ancient Black Egyptians knew enough mathematics to construct pyramids which even modern man cannot do. The teacher falsely made the statement that the ancient Egyptians were not Black and could not possibly have been the builders of the pyramids. To Jeff's mind the teacher implied that God made him inferior and he could not possibly achieve his goals. Jeff spent all day Saturday upset, wondering why God would have done that.

Sunday morning Jeff's parents made him go to Sunday School. The first thing Jeff saw was a big picture on the front wall of his classroom. The picture was labeled "Jesus Loves You" and the man in the picture was white. Another picture flashed back into Jeff's mind. It was the picture of his white male teacher who implied two days ago that God made him inferior. So what Jeff had struggled to reject all day Saturday was just confirmed by his own church. God is white, and He made Jeff inferior.

Our churches must understand the extent of their influence in shaping attitudes. The symbols and images we use can be significant in reinforcing societal views which have brainwashed our people. We must choose symbols and traditions which truly lead us into full development as God's children. As we study the Bible and world history and share knowledge about our past being uncovered by African American scholars, we can accurately document that God spoke through Black people in the Scriptures.

Ministry to families must be distinguished from merely giving sympathy and/or rescuing people from pain and/or advice–giving. Ministry builds relationships which encourage people to come to know and obey God through a personal, redemptive relationship with Jesus Christ. It empowers each family member. In ministering to African American families, it is important to deal with the unique issues which confront male/female relationships due to our historical experience as well as the special parenting issues which result from our status in this society.

Helping Couples Resolve Child Rearing Conflicts. Black men and women often differ in their approaches to child rearing. There are a variety of parenting styles. Some parents are authoritarian. They are "strict." Other parents prefer to work cooperatively with their child. As mentioned in the earlier chapter on parenting, these differences often cause conflict within marriages. Counselors can help couples see how these differences can complement each other and provide both the discipline and the nurturing support children need. Rather than seeing differences as reasons for conflict, the counselor can help couples see that "We are more of a person, more complete, with two sides." The complimentary of male and female roles is part of our tradition, unlike many other ethnic groups.

In counseling African American parents, it is important to emphasize that parents train boys and girls to assume a variety of adult roles. This is critical if the African American family of the future is to cope with social problems which the Black family will face. Families need to be aware of old habits, such as training boys to be more assertive than they train girls to be, and the problem that this may cause for girls who must function in future roles that will require more assertiveness and skill development.

Black families also may need to become aware of the tendency to encourage boys, in order to become males, to withdraw from emotional intimacy when they reach adolescence. Families need to be aware that, while adolescent females are encouraged to identify with parenting and nurturing, boys are not. This dual standard later causes conflict in marriages.

In order for counselors to encourage parents to set different goals for their children, they must also help parents see that the society through the media is working against them. For example, Black girls and boys are allowed to watch soap operas which present a definition of manhood that is usually not realistic for African American men or men in general. These cultural definitions are imprinted in their brains before the age of eight.

Few Black men are given the opportunity to achieve in the same ways that white men are projected as achieving. Whether they have college degrees or eighth grade educations only, Black men face unemployment more frequently than do white men.

Movement upward within their career is fraught with more obstacles.

Persons in family ministry should confront, discuss and deal with these realities, both with young people and with couples. These media images will continue to bring them into conflict with Black women who are not realistic. Continuous messages over television play up conflict between Black males and females through insults, power struggles, and demeaning behavior. Note the instruction of Scripture which can be applied to gender healing so needed among our people: Philippians 4:8; Ephesians 4:29.

Leaders in family ministry must also confront the problem that occurs when Black boys buy into the media images of determining the values of a woman by her physical beauty and not by her character. These images are usually cosmetic and include the notion that being beautiful means being blond and having blue eyes. These images also include the notion that real women stay at home and clean the house. They don't bring home part of the bacon.

It may require generations to change this type of Black male/Black female conflict. However, parents must be shown how to raise boys and girls who will be able to enter partnerships where both people work whether inside or outside of the home, and both people share responsibilities for raising children and keeping the home.

Family ministries must show parents how to prepare young people for the possibility that a woman may be earning more money than her husband. They must be shown how to raise girls who will someday help set financial goals for their families. They will want to raise girls and boys so that they respect one another regardless of income levels. Parents must be shown that they do young men a disservice if they raise them to be macho, unresponsive and unable to communicate with their wives.

Family ministries must help families by teaching them new skills of talking with one another, understanding one another, and working together. These are learned skills that must be taught. People are not born with them. They must be modeled and demonstrated repeatedly so that our people will internalize them.

Helping Couples Adjust to Differences in Ego States. Through counseling, a couple can be helped to see the three parts of a person that affect a marital relationship: parent, child and adult. The parental mode is more dominating. However, it can be caring and nurturing. Parents exact discipline and they tend to make decisions alone. Parents always teach. In the adult mode, however, a person desires independence from parents, responsibility, the freedom to reason and solve problems and the feeling of being mature. An adult desires mutuality and reciprocity. On the other hand, people who are acting within a child mode are more self–centered, irresponsible and dependent. They can also provide spontaneity and fun in a relationship.

Counselors can help clients examine a particular set of behaviors and identify the mode in which a particular partner is operating. Then counselors can help clients see how this relates to conflicts they may be experiencing in their marriages and family life.

Couples can actually visualize what it would be like for a male who is relating to his wife as a parent, and how this may force the wife to relate as a child. Counselors should avoid presenting this in terms of right and wrong. It should be examined in terms of what is. If husband and wife are happy with the parent/child relationship, and it functions well for them, then they have worked out a temporary solution at least.

A problem occurs when one of the partners changes because the original relationship no longer meets his/her needs. If the parent decides s/he wants to function as an adult, or the child decides that s/he wants to relate as an adult in spite of the fact that the partner doesn't agree with the change, conflict occurs. Through family ministry in the local church, couples can be helped to adjust their expectations so that they are able to operate in the mode best suited to their relationship and be flexible in their ego states.

Helping Couples Adjust to Changes in Female Roles. Many women are saying that they want more independence. In some ways, this is similar to moving from a child to an adult. Many Christian counselors are not equipped to deal with this type of conflict because they are not sure what the Bible says about it. Most counselors turn immediately to Ephesians the fifth chapter.

This passage says that wives are to submit to their husbands. However the passage also tells husbands to love their wives as Christ loved the church. Counselors must help husbands see that his role is not merely an authoritative one. The husband is more than a person who makes decisions. When a husband restricts his role to that of an authority figure, it produces conflict. This is particularly true among younger educated women who generally want shared decision making.

These conflicts can result from tensions between what a man believes is his scriptural responsibility and what he experiences in life. In helping men deal with these conflicts, family ministries emphasize the true meaning of marital roles. The relationship between husband and wife can be compared to that between Christ and believers. John 15:12–15 provides a principle that can help us understand this relationship:

"This is my commandment, That ye love one another, as I have loved you. Greater love hath no man than this, that a man lay down his life for his friends. Ye are my friends, if ye do whatsoever I command you. Henceforth I call you not servants; for the servant knoweth not what his lord doeth: but I have called you friends; for all things that I have heard of my Father I have made known unto you."

The inference that can be drawn from this passage is that the Lord has put us in a very special position. He is saying that Christians are not merely slaves who are commanded to do this and that, without reason or understanding. The basis of the relationship is love. Love forces a person to respect another and let the person know s/he is respected.

The person is not a slave, but a friend. Friendship suggests teamwork, collaboration, and cooperation based on respect. It is important for people to understand that, whenever the Scriptures talk about love, it is not in terms of feelings, but in terms of behavior. Love is always described in terms of attitudes and actions. This is in contrast to the definition given by the world of a fleeing, silly feeling. Love is not just a symbolic kind of emotional state. It consists of behavioral acts. That is how we know when love is present. It expresses itself in attitudes which are manifest in demonstrations and behavior which lead to the development and growth of another. Each expands as a result.

Encouraging Couples to Be Flexible. In Black families, everyone needs to work together in the context of love. Counselors can use this as a means for encouraging men and women to be flexible in assuming roles. This is particularly true if families are to cope with pressures now exerting themselves upon Black families. Uncles, aunts, cousins, and grandparents whether single or married have a part.

So often our families don't look or function as other families do. We have had an historical experience that has often led to the woman being employed and the man being unemployed. Across the nation, Black women have higher educational levels than Black men. This must be considered within the context of biblical principles if Black family life is to be more functional and stable, and if it is to accomplish the basic goals of family life. Counselors must help clients define leadership within the fundamental context of love and see roles within realistic options available to our families.

So often our families don't look structurally as other families do but many are functioning well, while others are struggling against significant odds. If within our churches we would assist each other with the tasks of family living, everyone would be enriched—young and old, educated and uneducated, men and women, poor and prosperous.

Summary. 1. The church is the living agency designated to not only evangelize, thereby spreading an accurate and complete portrayal of God's plan of salvation through Jesus Christ, but also to model and teach a redemptive way of life to its members and the society respectively.

2. The church must become the contemporary extended family where needed, bonding together believers through their commitment to spiritual values, mutual cooperation and accountability. This implies that the church will assume responsibility for leadership in fostering self–help in the African American community.

3. As in the days of old, the church/synagogue should be at the center of African American family life as a unifying moral force, an advocate in the larger society and a prophetic voice in a confused world. Therefore, from the church should emerge a paradigm of leadership, with a servant leader surrounded and held in check by a council of elders demonstrating the will and character of God in mission and decision making. As an advocate, the church should facilitate strong economic, educational, and political power in the Black community through training, monitoring and mediation.

4. The Scriptures must be interpreted and applied to the relevant needs of oppressed and fragmented families. This assumes that the African American church will exercise leadership in defining its theology, determining its priorities and rituals and developing organizational structures based on the history, experience and needs of Black people.

One would expect to see a proliferation of home–based Bible studies as Christians seriously and systematically study its content as related to their life experience. As part of that study is related to world history, they will discover that most of the people in the Old Testament were people of color. Equally interesting will be the similarity of biblical culture and African cultures.

5. The present–day church is challenged to conceptualize its mission to include preparing the family in all areas of its life. Since many Black families can no longer adequately

carry out those functions as economic conditions worsen, this will become increasingly difficult for more families. Good nutrition, safe and adequate housing, and healthy bodies and minds provide the building blocks for full growth and development. Churches should be open seven days a week offering schools, infant day care, counseling, senior citizen activities, parenting classes, tutorials, and study groups. The church's learning center can feature health fairs, job banks, legal clinics, recovery and alcohol/drug rehabilitation groups, camps, and youth activities—a home away from home. This describes our vision of outreach for the church. This holistic approach will find the church offering some of these ministries directly, collaborating with other groups in making some available and referring members to existing resources for still others. The end result should be greater unity within the African American religious community.

6. Family ministry means creating a supportive community for all who enter the gates. Conscious effort to build congregations which include all income groups, ages, educational levels and backgrounds is true kingdom building and involves an inclusive community of singles, single parents, dual career holders, parents, and grandparents. Each is respected and valued and contributing their uniqueness to the whole.

7. Discipleship/character education should be available for all members of the family in an ongoing, systematic manner in order to equip parents, children, teenagers, singles and other members of the extended family, including uncles and aunts. Rites of passage programs would be conducted for boys and girls preparing and ushering them into adulthood. This education, including knowledge of our African history and cultural heritage will provide a tool for identity resolution (Who am I? What is my place in the world?) and goal clarification (What is my part? How do I contribute to what has gone before?), resulting in hope and direction for the future.

Equipping the African American family for the 21st century will not be easy. Fear of hard work should not lead one to adopt the attitude that we are God's children, therefore one can sit back and wait on God to make things all right. To do this would reflect a lack of understanding of the partnership between God and man that He has set forth.

If we know God, understand Him and remain faithful in obeying the Word, He in fact will guide us to accomplish the mission. The Holy Spirit will help us minister to one another, assist in the transformation of each other's minds and strengthen the family.

This chapter has stressed the importance of understanding the roles society has defined for us and the criticalness of defining our own goals and roles. The chapter also pinpointed the need to train our children for the roles we have defined for them to assume. This can be done effectively in church–based family ministry for African Americans.

The following exercise provides an opportunity to apply some of the information presented in this chapter to analyzing a biblical family.

BIBLE FAMILIES

INSTRUCTIONS: Jesus was in the ministry of healing hurting families. The following exercises provide the opportunity to study families that Jesus touched. The first five exercises consist of five "fill–in–the–blank" discovery exercises and a summary question. The sixth exercise provides an opportunity to apply the knowledge gained to a family ministry. The seventh exercise allows for personal application.

Jesus' Family

"Now the birth of Jesus Christ was on this wise: When as his mother Mary was espoused to Joseph, before they came together, she was found with child of the Holy Ghost. Then Joseph being raised from sleep

did as the angel of the Lord had bidden him, and took unto him his wife: And knew her not till she had brought forth her firstborn son: and he called his name Jesus." (Matthew 1:18, 24–25)

The Family of Lazarus

"Then said Martha unto Jesus, Lord, if thou hadst been here, my brother had not died. But I know, that even now, whatsoever thou wilt ask of God, God will give it thee. And said, Where have ye laid him? They said unto him, Lord, come and see. Jesus wept. And when he thus had spoken, he cried with a loud voice, Lazarus, come forth. And he that was dead came forth..." (John 11:21–22, 34–35, 43–44)

The Newlyweds

"And the third day there was a marriage in Cana of Galilee; and the mother of Jesus was there; And when they wanted wine, the mother of Jesus saith unto him, They have no wine. Jesus saith unto them, Fill the water-pots with water...When the ruler of the feast had tasted the water that was made wine...The governor of the feast called the bridegroom, And saith unto him...thou hast kept the good wine until now." (John 2:1, 3, 7, 9–10)

The Widow of Nain

"And it came to pass the day after, that he went into a city called Nain; and many of his disciples went with him, and much people. Now when he came nigh to the

gate of the city, behold, there was a dead man carried out, the only son of his mother, and she was a widow: and much people of the city was with her.

"And when the Lord saw her, he had compassion on her, and said unto her, Weep not. And he came and touched the bier: and they that bare him stood still. And he said, Young man, I say unto thee, Arise. And he that was dead sat up, and began to speek. And he delivered him to his mother." (Luke 7:11–15)

Publius

"In the same quarters were possessions of the chief man of the island, whose name was Publius; who received us, and lodged us three days courteously. And it came to pass, that the father of Publius lay sick of a fever and of a bloody flux: to whom Paul entered in, and prayed, and laid his hands on him, and healed him. So when this was done, others also, which had diseases in the island, came, and were healed: Who also honoured us with many honours; and when we departed, they laded us with such things as were necessary." (Acts 28:7–10)

1. Jesus Touches His Family (Matthew 1:18, 24–25)

Scripture indicates that Jesus had quite an impact on His personal family.

a. In what ways was Joseph affected by having come into contact with Jesus? (Luke 1:27; 2:4; 3:23; Matthew 1:18, 24; 2:1–23; Luke 2:41–51)

b. In what ways was Mary affected by having come into contact with Jesus? (Luke 1:26–56; 2:1, 7; Matthew 2:11–23; 12:46–50; John 2:1–4; 12; 19:25–27; Acts 1:14)

c. In what ways were Jesus' brothers and sisters affected by having come into contact with Him? (Matthew 13:55, 56; Mark 6:3; 3:21, 31; John 7:3–5; Acts 1:13, 14)

d. In what ways were Jesus' cousins and other relatives affected by having come into contact with Him? (Luke 1:36–56; 3:19; Matthew 3:5, 15; 14:3–12; John 3:23; 4:1; 7:19–28; Mark 6:17–29)

e. Peter, James and John were the three apostles most frequently mentioned in proximity to our Lord in His ministry. How was this "surrogate family" affected by having come into contact with Jesus? (Acts 1)

f. SUMMARY QUESTION: From the life of Jesus, what can be learned about the potential impact of a committed Christian's life on his/her family?

2. Jesus in the Lives of Mary, Martha, and Lazarus (John 11:1–44)

This famous family changed as a result of knowing Jesus.

a. In what way was Mary changed, as a result of having come into contact with Jesus? (Luke 10:38–42; Matthew 26:6–13)

b. How was Martha changed as a result of having come into contact with Jesus? (Luke 10:38, 42; John 11:1–39; 12:2)

c. How was Lazarus changed as a result of having come into contact with Jesus? (John 11:1–44; 12:1–10)

d. In what ways was this family a "family" to Jesus? (John 11:1–44)

e. How were other people affected by Jesus' ministry with this family? (John 11:45–53)

f. SUMMARY QUESTION: Each person in Lazarus' family had a similar, but unique testimony. What lessons can be learned about the potential impact of family ministry on a whole neighborhood or community?

3. Jesus Touches Newlyweds (John 2:1–11)

Jesus performed a miracle very early in the life of a newlywed couple in Cana of Galilee.

a. What evidence is there that the members of the newlyweds' extended family were friends of Jesus' family? (John 2:1–2)

b. What was the immediate problem that Jesus was called upon to address? (2:3)

c. Why did Jesus answer His mother in the way He did? (2:4) What was her response? (2:5)

d. Describe the miracle that took place. (2:7–9)

e. What was the object lesson that Jesus taught this family? (2:9–11)

f. SUMMARY QUESTION: What lessons can be learned from Jesus' interaction with this newlywed couple and their extended family? How does this story relate to modern families?

4. Jesus Touches Families Through Children (Luke 7:11–15)

By healing children, Jesus reached their adult relatives.

a. Explain how adults may have been reached through the life of an official's son? (John 4:46–54)

b. Explain how a widow may have been reached after witnessing the experience of her child with Jesus. (Luke 7:11–15)

c. Explain how another woman may have been reached after witnessing the experience of her child with Jesus. (Matthew 15:21–28; Mark 7:24–30)

d. Explain how Jairus must have been affected after witnessing his daughter's experience with Jesus. (Matthew 9:18–26; Mark 5:22–24, 35–43; Luke 8:41–42, 49–56)

e. Explain how the relatives of the epileptic boy must have reacted after observing the boy's experience with Jesus. (Matthew 17:14–18; Mark 9:17–27; Luke 9:37–42)

f. SUMMARY QUESTION: What implications do the above

stories have for evangelizing through Vacation Bible School?

5. Jesus Touches Families—the Book of Acts (Acts 28:7–10)

After the ascension of Jesus into heaven and the gift of the Holy Spirit, Jesus continued to touch and heal families.

a. Who was Publius and how might his relatives have been affected after hearing of Jesus' healing Publius' father? (Acts 28:7–10) How was the surrounding community affected?

b. How might the family of Dorcas have been affected after observing her healing? (Acts 9:36–41)

c. How might the family of Eutychus have been affected after hearing and/or witnessing his healing? (Acts 20:7–12)

d. How might the family of the lame man at the gate of the temple have responded to hearing and/or witnessing his healing? (Acts 3:1–19)

e. How might Aeneas' family have been affected by hearing and/or witnessing his healing? (Acts 9:32–35)

f. SUMMARY QUESTION: What lessons can be learned from biblical families about ministering to hurting people in communities surrounding churches?

6. FAMILY MINISTRY APPLICATION

What lesson can be learned about the renewal of families through Jesus Christ? How can this information be used when ministering to families through the church?

7. PERSONAL APPLICATION

Do you have a hurt that Jesus needs to heal? Pray that He will heal you, and then through you, heal people who are hurting in your family.

RESOURCES

Abatso, George and Yvonne. *The Black Christian Family* (Chicago: Urban Ministries, Inc., 1985).

Adams, Jay E. *Marriage, Divorce and Remarriage* (Grand Rapids: Zondervan, 1980).

Akbar, Na'im. *Chains and Images of Psychological Slavery* (Tallahassee, Florida: New Mind Press, 1984).

Applewhite, Barry. *Find Yourself-Give Yourself* (Wheaton: Victor Books, 1980).

Backus, William and Marie Chapian. *Telling Yourself the Truth* (Bloomington, Minnesota: Bethany Fellowship, Inc., 1980).

Bauer, David G. *The "How To" Grants Manual* (New York: Macmillan Publishing Company, 1984).

Ben-Jochannon, Y. *Black Man on the Nile and His Family* (New York: Alkebu-Ian Books, 1981).

Ben-Jochannon, Y. *African Origins of the Major "Western Religions"* (New York: Alkebu-lan Books, 1970).

Bradley, M. *The Iceman Inheritance: Prehistoric Sources of Western Racism, Sexism and Aggression* (New York: Warner Books, 1981).

Brothers, Joyce. "Why Husbands Walk Out," *Reader's Digest,* July 1987, pp. 27-32.

Brown, Addie H. "Ancient Kemetic Family Caring and Sharing Attitudes," *Reconstructing Kemetic Culture,* Maulana Karenga (Los Angeles: University of Sankoree Press, 1990).

Bustanoby, Andrea. "Sharing a Sensitive, Sensible Heart: A Counselor Tells What to Do When Your Child is Depressed," *Fundamental Journal,* Volume 5, No. 4, April, 1986, pp. 30-32.

Carter, Velma Thorne and J. Lynn Leavenworth. *Caught in the Middle: Children of Divorce* (Valley Forge: Judson Press, 1985).

Christopherson, Victor A. *Childrearing in Today's Christian Family* (Valley Forge: Judson Press, 1985).

Clark, Reginald. *Black Family Achievement in School* (Chicago: University of Chicago Press, 1983).

Crabb, Lawrence. *Basic Principles of Biblical Counseling* (Grand Rapids: Zondervan Press, 1975).

Crabb, Lawrence, Jr. *Effective Biblical Counseling* (Grand Rapids: Zondervan Press, 1977).

D'Antonio, William V., and Joan Aldous. *Families and Religion: Conflict and Change in Modern Society.* Conference Papers, University of Notre Dame, 1981, p. 320 (Beverly Hills California: Sage Publications, 1983).

Davis, Ernest, Jr., D.Min. *Utilizing the Local Church as a Non-Traditional Setting for the Delivery of Mental Health Services* (Drew University, 1983). Dissertation Abstracts International, Volume 44/11-A, p. 3411 (ORDER NO: AAD84-02915).

Dennis, Ruth E. "Social Stress and Mortality Among Non-white Males," *Phylon,* Volume 38, No. 3, September, 1977, pp. 315-328.

Diop, Cheikh A. *The Cultural Unity of Black Africa* (Chicago: Third World Press, 1978).

Diop, Cheikh A. *The African Origin of Civilization* (Westport: Lawrence Hill and Co., 1974).

Doering, Jeanne. *The Power of Encouragement* (Chicago: Moody Press, 1982).

Eng, Eugenia, John Callan, and Anne Callan. "Institutionalizing Social Support through the Church and into the Community," *Health Education Quarterly,* Volume 12, No. 1, Spring, 1985, pp. 81-92.

Estadt, B. K., Siang-Yang Tan, Emerson, James Gordon. "Lay Pastoral Counseling: Thought and Response," *Journal of Pastoral Care,* Volume 40, No. 4, December, 1986, pp. 291, 304-309.

Fleshch, Rudolf. *Why Johnny Can't Read* (New York: Harper & Row, 1955).

Freidman, Maurice. "Healing Through Meeting," *Tikkum,* Volume 3, March-April, 1988, pp. 33-35, 85-87.

Fryling, Alice. *An Unequal Yoke* (Downers Grove: Intervarsity Press, 1979).

Gaulke, Earl H. *You Can Have a Family Where Everybody Wins* (St Louis: Concordia Press, 1987).

Gee, Arizona Langston. *Viewpoints of a Black Senior Citizen* (Seminole: Open Door Ministries, 1986).

Gilkes, Cheryl Towsend. "The Black Church as a Therapeutic Community: Suggested Areas for Research into the Black Religious Experience," *Journal of the Interdenominational Theological Center,* 8, Fall 1980, pp. 29-44.

Goba, Bonganjalo. "The Role of the Black Church in the Process of Healing Human Brokenness: A Perspective in Pastoral Theology," *Journal of Theology of South Africa,* September, 1979, No. 28, pp. 7-13.

Griffith, Ezra E. "The Impact of Culture and Religion on Psychiatric Care," Yale U School of Medicine, *Journal of the National Medical Association,* Vol. 74 (12), December, 1982, pp. 1175-1179. ISSN: 00279684.

Hale-Benson, Janice. *Black Children* (Baltimore: Johns Hopkins University, 1982).

Hare, Julia and Nathan. *Bringing the Black Boy to Manhood* (San Francisco: Black Think Tank, 1984).

Hare, Nathan and Julia. *Endangered Black Family* (San Francisco: Black Think Tank, 1985).

Harris, Thomas A. *I'm OK, You're OK* (New York: Harper and Row, 1973).

Hawk, Gary. *Building Bonds Between Adults and Their Aging Parents* (Nashville: Convention Press, 1987).

Heath, Daryl. *Counseling Children About Christian Conversion and Church Membership* (Nashville: Southern Baptist Sunday School Board, 1975).

Henning, Lawrence H. "The Emotional Aspect of Treating Child Abuse," *Journal of Religion and Health,* Spring, 1987, 26:37-42.

Hodges, Norman. *The Senior Years: Getting There/Being There* (Nashville: Southern Baptist Convention Publishing Board, 1983).

Hollyday, Joyce. "The Nightmare of Abuse," *Sojourner,* Volume 17, February 1988, pp. 5-6.

Hopson, D. and Hopson, D. *Different and Wonderful: Raising Black Children in a Race-Conscious Society* (New York: Prentice Hall, 1990).

Jackson, Jacquelyne Johnson. "Contemporary Relationships Between Black Families and Black Churches in the United States: A Speculative Inquiry," in *Families and Religions,* edited by W. D'Antonio and J. Aldous, 1983, pp. 191-220.

Jackson, John G. *Introduction to African Civilization* (Secaucus: The Citadel Press, 1980).

Jackson, John G. *Man, God and Civilization* (New York: Grove Press, 1971).

James, George. *Stolen Legacy* (San Francisco: Julian Richardson & Assoc., 1976).

Jones, R. L. *Black Psychology* (New York: Harper & Row, 1972).

Jones, Stephen D. *Faith Shaping Nurturing the Faith Journey of Youth* (Valley Forge, Pa: Judson Press, 1980).

Jourard, Sidney M. *The Transparent Self* (D. Van Nostrand Co., Inc., 1964).

Kantzer, Kenneth S. and Paul Fromer. "Nightmare of the 80's: Despite Its Disastrous Effects, the Use of Cocaine is Skyrocketing," *Christianity Today,* Volume 30, No. 4, March 7, 1986, 14-15.

Karenga, Maulana. *Introduction to Black Studies* (Los Angeles: Kawaida Publishers, 1982).

Knight, George W. *When Families Hurt, Deacons Can Help* (Nashville: Southern Baptist Sunday School Board, 1976).

Kunjufu, Jawanza. *Countering the Conspiracy to Destroy Black Boys* (Chicago: African American Images, 1985).

_____. *Developing Positive Self-Images and Discipline in Black Children* (Chicago: African American Images, 1984).

_____. *Lessons from History: A Celebration in Blackness* (Chicago: African American Images, 1987).

_____. *Motivating and Preparing Black Youth to Work* (Chicago: African American Images, 1986).

_____. *To Be Popular or Smart: The Black Peer Group* (Chicago: African American Images, 1988).

La Haye, Timothy F. and Beverly LaHaze. "Help Your Teen Avoid Suicide," *Fundamentalist Journal,* Volume 5, No. 1, January, 1986, p. 59.

Larson, Jim. *A Church Guide for Strengthening Families* (Columbus: Augsburg, 1986).

Lawson, William B. "Chronic Mental Illness and the Black Family," *American Journal of Social Psychiatry,* Volume 6, No. 1, Winter, 1986, pp. 57-61.

Lewis, Mary. *Herstory: Black Female Rites of Passage* (Chicago: African American Images, 1988).

Lincoln, Eric C. "Black Family, The Black Church, and The Transformation of Values," *Religious Life,* Volume 47, Winter, 1978, pp. 486-496.

Livezey, Louis Gehr. "Sexual and Family Violence: A Growing Issue for the Churches," *Christian Century,* October 28, 1987, 104:938-942.

Lloyd, Anthony Frazier, D.Min. *The Black Church's Role in Community Mental Health Care* (School of Theology at Claremont, 1985). Dissertation Abstracts International, Volume 46/06-A, p. 1650 (ORDER NO: AAD85-16146).

Lorch, Barbara. "Church Youth Alcohol and Drug Education Programs," *Journal of Religion and Health,* Summer 1987, 26:106-114.

Lundberg, Sherry. "Ministering to Victims of Domestic Violence," *Christian Ministry,* March, 1987, 18:25-27.

Lyles, Michael R. and James H. Carter. "Myths and Strengths of the Black Family: A Historical and Sociological Contribution to Family Therapy," *Journal of the National Medical Association,* Vol. 74 (11), Nov., 1982, pp. 1119-1123.

Mace, David and Vera Mace. *Letters to a Retired Couple* (Valley Forge: Judson Press, 1985).

McCray, Walter. *Reaching and Teaching Young Black Adults* (Chicago: Black Light Fellowship, 1985).

McDowell, Josh. *Building Your Self-Image* (Wheaton: Tyndale House Publishers, 1987).

Monroe, Doris D. *Reaching and Teaching Mentally Retarded Persons* (Nashville: Convention Press, 1980).

Murray, Robert G., D.Min. *The Black Alcoholic In and Out of the Black Church* (Boston: Boston University School of Theology, 1981).

Nabi, Gene. *Ministering to Persons with Mental Retardation and Their Families* (Nashville: Convention Press, 1985).

234

Neer, Tom. "Neighbors Without Shelter in the Trauma of Homeless Families," *Sojourner,* June, 1988, 17:34-35.

Norwood, Robin. *Women Who Care Too Much* (New York: Pocket Books, 1985).

Nowen, Henri. *The Wounded Healer* (New York: Image Books, 1979).

Ogilvie, Lloyd J. *You Are Loved and Forgiven* (Ventura, California: Regal Books, 1987).

Oglesby, William B. "Referral as Pastoral Care," *Journal of Pastoral Care,* June 1987, 41:176-187.

Olander, E.A. "Amends: Abusive Men Exploring New Directions," *Military Chaplain's Review,* Spring 1986, No. 2, 43-52.

Olson, Richard, and Carole Della Pia-Terry. *Help for Remarried Couples and Families* (Valley Forge: Judson Press, 1985).

Osei, G. K. *African Contributions to Civilization* (London: African Publication Society, 1973).

Patterson, George W. "The Pastoral Care of Persons in Pain," *Journal of Religion and Aging,* Fall 1984, No. 1, 17-30.

Perkins, John. *A Call to Holistic Ministry* (Seminole, Florida: Open Door Ministries, 1975).

Pipe, Virginia. *Live and Learn with Your Teenager* (Valley Forge: Judson Press, 1985).

Powell, John. *Why Am I Afraid to Tell You Who I Am* (Saratoga Springs: Argus Communications, 1987).

Pressley, Arthur L., Jr. *A Study in the Use of Consumer Marketing Theory to Develop Entry Systems for Pastoral Counseling Centers* (Northwestern University, Dissertation Abstracts International, 1986). Volume 47/06-A, p. 2202.

Richardson, Bernard Lester, Ph.D. *The Attitudes of Black Clergy and Parishioners Toward Mental Illness and Mental Health Professionals* (Michigan State University, 1981). Dissertation Abstracts International, Volume 43/02-B, p. 512 (ORDER NO: AAD82-16583).

Rodgers, Augustus and Edward D. Hayes. "Development of a Counseling and Referral Service in a Black Church," *Psychiatric Forum,* Volume 12, No. 2, Spring 1984, pp. 48-52.

Rodney, W. *How Europe Underdeveloped Africa* (Washington: Howard University Press, 1974).

Rogers, J. A. *Africa's Gift to America* (New York: Helga Rogers, 1961).

Rogers, J. A. *Sex and Race,* Vols. 1, 2, 3 (New York: Helga Rogers, 1980).

Rogers, J. A. *A World's Great Men of Color,* Vols. 1, 2 (New York: Collier Books, 1972).

Ross, Sharon Zanter. "A Pastoral Response to Incest: Theological Resources for Those Who Care for Victims and Victimizers," *Lutheran Forum,*

February 21, 1987, No 2:12-18.

Saint George, Arthur and Patrick H. McNamara. "Religion, Race and Psychological Well-Being," *JSSR,* Volume 23, December, 1984, pp. 351-363.

Schaper, Richard. "Pastoral Care for Persons with AIDS and Their Families," *Christian Century,* August 12-19, 1987, 104:691-694.

Schlesinger, Benjamin. "Abuse of the Elderly is the Silent Crime," *Grail,* March, 1988, 4:53-61.

Simms, Claudette. *Don't Weep for Me* (Houston: Impressions, 1989).

Smith, Archie. *The Relational Self: Ethics and Therapy from a Black Church Perspective* (Nashville: Abingdon Press, 1982).

Smith, W. C. *The Church in the Life of the Black Family* (Valley Forge: Judson Press, 1987).

Smith, Wallace Charles. *A Family Enrichment Curriculum for the Black Church* (Eastern Baptist Theological Seminary, 1979). Dissertation Abstracts International, Volume 40/03-A, p. 529.

Sontag, Frederick E. "Evil, Being Black, and Love," *Journal of the Inter-denominational Theological Center,* Volume 10, No. 1-2, Fall-Spring, 1982-83, pp. 15-19.

Spotts, Dwight and Veerman, David. *Reaching Out to Troubled Youth* (Wheaton: Victor Books, 1987).

Stafford, Tim. *The Sexual Christian* (Wheaton: Victor Books, 1987).

Stoner, Thomas K. "Family Life Education in the Local Church," *Christian Education Journal,* 1984, Volume 5, No. 2, pp. 53-56.

Strunk, Orlo, Jr. "The Therapeutic Use of Devotional Reading in Working with the Aging," *Journal of Religion and Aging,* No. 2, 1-8, Winter, 1984.

Tatum, Beverly Daniel, Ph.D. *Life in Isolation: Black Families Living in a Predominantly White Community* (The University of Michigan, 1984). Dissertation Abstracts International, Volume 45/07-B, p. 2365 (ORDER NO: AAD84-22337).

Thomas, Robert, D.Min. *Alternative Strategies for Inner-City Black Churches in Ministry to the Black Youth Job Crisis* (San Francisco Theological Seminary, 1973). Dissertation Abstracts International, Volume X1973.

Van Meter, Mary Jane S. and Patricia Johnson. "Family Decision-making and Long-Term Care for the Elderly," *Journal of Religion and Aging,* No. 4, Summer, 1985, pp. 59-72.

Van Sertima, Ivan. *Blacks in Science: Ancient and Modern* (New Brunswick: The Journal of African Civilization, 1983).

Van Sertima, Ivan. *Egypt Revisited* (New Brunswick: The Journal of African Civilization, 1989).

Van Sertima, Ivan. *Great African Thinkers,* Vol. 1 (New Brunswick: The Journal of African Civilization, 1986).

Van Sertima, Ivan. *Nile Valley Civilizations* (New Brunswick: The Journal of African Civilization, 1985).

Van Sertima, Ivan. *They Came Before Columbus* (New York: Random House, 1976).

Vann, Fred Herbert, D.Min. *Developing a Functional Program for the Black Church in Pastoral Care Through Working Together of the Clergy and the Laity* (Boston University School of Theology, 1985).

Walker, Curtis. "A Christian Perspective of God and Suffering, Particularly in Family Violence/Spouse Abuse," *AME Zion Quarterly Review,* October, 1987, pp. 22-37.

Walker, David. *David Walker's Appeals,* Charles Wiltse (Ed.) (New York: Hill and Wang, 1978).

Wedel, Leonard E. *Making the Most of Retirement* (Nashville: Southern Baptist Convention Publishing Board, 1976).

Wiggen, Cooper. "The Male Minister and the Female Rape Victim," *Christian Ministry,* May, 1987, 18:24-26.

Williams, Chancellor. *The Destruction of Black Civilization* (New York: Third World Press, 1974).

Williams, Charles, Jr. "Contemporary Voluntary Associations in the Urban Black Church: The Development and Growth of Mutual Aid Societies," *Journal of Voluntary Action Research,* Volume 13, No. 4, Oct.-Dec., 1984, 19-30.

Williams, James H. "Back to Basics: A New Challenge for the Black Church," *Explorations in Ethnic Studies,* 1980, 3(1):13-18.

Wilson, Amos. *Developmental Psychology of the Black Child* (Chicago: African American Images, 1978).

Wilson, Earl D. "Ministering to Victims of Incest," *Leadership,* Volume 9, Winter 1988, pp. 127-129.

Wimberly, Edward P. *Pastoral Care in the Black Church* (Nashville: Abingdon Press, 1979).

Wimberly, Edward P. *Pastoral Counseling and Spiritual Values* (Nashville: Abingdon Press, 1982).

Woods, John Henry, Jr., D.Min. *The Black Church in the Ministry of Housing* (American Baptist Seminary of the West, 1981). Dissertation Abstracts International, Volume X1981.

Woodson, Carter G. *The Miseducation of the Negro* (Washington, D.C.: Associated Publishers, 1933).

Worthington, Everett L. *How to Help the Hurting* (Downer's Grove: Intervarsity Press, 1985).

Wright, H. Norman. *Crisis Counseling: Helping People in Crisis and Stress* (San Bernadino, California: Here's Life Publishers, 1985).

Wyatt, Lawrence Paul, D.Min. *Developing a Premarital Guidance Pro-*

gram within a Group of Black Local Churches of God in the Detroit, Michigan Area (Drew University, 1982). Dissertation Abstracts International, Volume 43/10-A, p. 3280.

The following sources should be able to assist you in locating any of the above books:

Black Images Book Bazaar
P. O. Box 41059
Dallas, TX 75241

Bridges Book Center
1480 Main Street
Rahway, NJ 07065

Know Book Store
306 S. Dillard Street
Durham, NC 27701

The Shrine of the Black Madonna Bookstore
946 Gordon Street, S.W.
Atlanta, GA 30310

Urban Ministries, Inc.
1350 W. 103rd Street
Chicago, IL 60643

Urban Ministries, Inc., of Chicago, Illinois is an independent Christian publishing company formed in 1970. UMI is the first predominantly African American–owned publisher to produce interdenominational Sunday School and Vacation Bible School curriculum.

UMI also produces Christian video products which have earned several awards including the "Chicago Emmy" and the "Angel Award."